The LESSONS of ALOHA

STORIES OF THE HUMAN SPIRIT

The LESSONS of ALOHA

STORIES OF THE HUMAN SPIRIT

with Brother Noland

photography by Shuzo Uemoto

WATERMARK PUBLISHING

Editors
Arnold Hiura
George Engebretson

Book design and production
Gonzalez Design Company

Library of Congress Catalog Number: 99-75822
ISBN 0-9631154-8-0

Watermark Publishing
1000 Bishop Street, Suite 501-A
Honolulu, Hawaii 96813
Telephone: (808) 587-7766

Printed in China

To my daughters
Charis Pomaikaʻimahina
Erika-Rae Keahiamauloaokanoholani
Brooke Ligaya Keʻiliahipua

And to Sandee,
for all your contributions to the community
around us and the world at large. May you realize
all the dreams and goals of your journey and,
along the way, respect the path that is mine.

Brother Noland

Brother Noland is a Native Hawaiian musician with an international reputation as an artist and teacher. He is an acclaimed ki hoʻalu (slack key) guitarist, a prolific recording artist and a composer of scores for film and television. His professional and community honors include multiple Na Hoku Hanohano and Billboard awards, the State of Hawaiʻi proclamation of Brother Noland Day in September 1997, and inclusion in the Variety Club of Hawaii's Celebrity Circle at King's Village. He works extensively with youth and senior groups, conducting workshops in ki hoʻalu and ukulele and sharing his Hawaiian heritage and cultural values. Among his other accomplishments, Brother Noland founded the Kalihi-Pālama Settlement Performing Arts Program in 1993.

Shuzo Uemoto

The photography of Shuzo Uemoto exhibits a strong sense of concern for the people of Hawaiʻi. He has won wide acclaim, both in Hawaiʻi and abroad, for his unconventional printmaking methods and for his culturally sensitive portraits of Hawaii's hula resources in the two-volume "Na Na I Na Loea Hula," published by the Kalihi-Pālama Culture and Arts Society. Shuzo is the staff photographer for the Honolulu Academy of Arts and a lecturer in art at Kapiʻolani Community College. His children, Maya and Kekua, are his constant reminders of the joy of seeing rainbows and the everyday lessons of Aloha.

Contents

Acknowledgments

Aloha to all the wonderful people who offered their unconditional love, thoughts and truths to **The Lessons of Aloha**.

Aloha to the fine creative team that produced this book: George Engebretson, Arnold Hiura, Shuzo Uemoto and Leo Gonzalez. Thank you for translating the music of my thoughts and feelings onto the printed page.

Aloha, Duane Kurisu, for bringing my imagination to reality. We share the same vision and fly the same airplane.

Salamat, Frank Mamalias, my greatest inspiration and mentor along the path of the peaceful warrior. You have taught me the inner spiritual essence that keeps my journey and life force ever moving, without fear.

Aloha, Walter Ritte, Jr., for returning me to the Earth Mother and sharing with me the universal wisdom of the Hawaiians.

Aloha, Rex Nimoto, for the constant and the change. Your healing is my music.

Aloha, Kaipo Daniels, the first to notice that "the boy can hold a tune." You taught me the song of the heart. This book is a reflection of your Aloha.

Aloha, Dad. I have always known you.

Aloha, Tony, Keahi and Mom, for our dreams, our sacrifices and our moments together.

Aloha to Steve Bader, Tony Conjugacion, Shannon Crivello, Janis Okino, Mele Look, George Kam, Kimo Rodrigues, Heidi Ho, Bob Omura, Bob Rath, Jackie Rath, Eloise Nakama, Donnie Martin, Jr., Keala Campton, Joe Lee, Lori Buchanan, Kim Fook Kam, MBFT Media and all the others who contributed so selflessly to **The Lessons of Aloha**.

Brother Noland
Honolulu, Hawai'i

Preface

We can learn a lot from our neighbors, especially in Hawai'i, a community made up of so many different cultures from all over the world. The everyday people you'll meet in this book have wonderful stories to tell—as dramatic as a hostage situation, as soft as the power of prayer. But big or small, each one is a story with a message.

The sharing of human experience is a great way to make a point. It's what Hawaiian visionary Kenny Brown—he's on page 66—calls "teaching without preaching." And if Hawaii's people have much to teach each other, they also have some universal truths to share with the rest of the world—lessons in living that make good sense whether your home island is Maui or Manhattan.

It all comes down to how we can best live the spirit of Aloha. There are lots of different versions of Aloha, from the classic dictionary definition—"in the presence of divine breath"—to the tour guide's hearty "Alo-o-o-ha!" The fact is, there's no single answer to the meaning of Aloha—except for its foundation in Love. The stories here are all different takes on the Aloha spirit—each conveying the message in its own way.

The storytellers in **The Lessons of Aloha** represent a broad cross-section of today's Hawai'i—teachers and coaches, students and shopkeepers, artists and entrepreneurs, healers and heroes. Together, these people take us on a journey of discovery—and offer some important tools for living along the way.

To lead us on this Island safari, there could be no better native guide than Brother Noland. This popular musician and recording artist also works tirelessly on behalf of senior citizens and disadvantaged children. He has dreamed of creating a book like this for many years; it has been a pleasure to help him make that dream come true.

Likewise, Shuzo Uemoto was a natural choice as the book's photographer. His sensitive portraits in these pages convey their own fine sense of the human spirit.

We hope you enjoy **The Lessons of Aloha.** Most of all, we hope you find inspiration in its message, as you share these stories with your family and friends.

Aloha,
Duane K. Kurisu

Introduction

T his book has no real beginning, middle or end. Rather, it's a treasury of personal stories shared by 40 very special people—all of them Hawai'i folks I've been fortunate enough to meet along my life's journey. They are mentors, teachers, wisdom keepers and survivors—new friends as well as old. I'm honored that these ordinary people have consented to share their extraordinary stories in these pages. Their voices offer timeless, priceless lessons to live by—guideposts to understanding ourselves and our connection with Hawai'i and the rest of the world.

This much I have learned: the ability to help, to inspire and to improve our quality of life resides in each of us—regardless of our age, occupation, gender, ethnicity or economic status. The remarkable variety of people who have contributed to this book stands as testimony to that fact.

Like a cultural magnet, Hawai'i has attracted many diverse people to its shores. The first were Polynesian, of course, but today we are many different ethnic groups—each contributing its own culture, style and wisdom to the whole. How we all manage to get along with each other is commonly attributed to the Aloha spirit. But what exactly is Aloha?

To find out, I set out to explore the heart and soul of the Islands—its ethnic rainbow of races and faces. The idea for this book was born more than five years ago. Even then it was clear that the dawn of the new millennium would foster many publications, but I felt that the uniqueness of this book would reside in the people we gathered together. If they could tell their stories of survival in our challenging world, if we could feel their passion for life, then this book would be a gift we could share not only with others in Hawai'i, but with people the world over. It's all done local style—simple and honest, yet universal.

On Moloka'i, Brother Noland contemplates the view from the Kalaupapa Overlook.

"Aloha is not just some words on a sign. It's something you feel from inside. So... I want to help you feel my Aloha. I know you can feel it like me It's here in your heart."

—from *The Aloha Song* by Erika-Rae, Brooke Ligaya and Brother Noland

Brother Noland talks story with friends and mentors, including Boogie Kahilihiwa (below, at Kalaupapa), Frank Mamalias (bottom) and Auntie Mae Akeo Brown at the Kodak Hula Show.

Our quest to talk story with and to photograph these individuals in their own surroundings took us from the high-rises of urban Honolulu to the rainswept Kohala Mountains on the Big Island. In between, we found ourselves sharing ideas on a Kalihi football field (with John Sharp), on the bleachers at the Kodak Hula Show (Auntie Mae Brown), in a personal dojo (Atsuo Nishioka), on a fishing boat at Kewalo Basin (Jonathan Lee) and in a host of other places thoughout the Islands. We talked over a barbed wire fence with rancher Charlie Onaka, took a rock wall tour with builder Ralph Soken and sampled Big Island Candies with businessman Allan Ikawa.

Certainly our most moving experience came in the isolated Moloka'i settlement of Kalaupapa. There we were privileged to meet some of the wonderful folks who make Kalaupapa their home. I'll never forget the overwhelming wave of emotion that washed over me as we entered Auntie Katherine Puahala's house. It was like going back in time. Everything was in

its proper place, as if it had all been there forever. It was May, but her little Christmas tree remained decorated. "Every day is Christmas," she explained. Auntie Katherine was a little guarded at first, as if she was feeling out where I was coming from. She–like the other two kūpuna we interviewed at Kalaupapa–had never spoken for publication before. Once she felt comfortable with us, her stories poured out for nearly five hours, like an epic movie filled with drama and Aloha. As we left, physically drained, our eyes swollen with tears, we felt stronger than ever our great responsibility in creating this book.

Another day we interviewed one of my most revered advisers, Frank Mamalias, at his workplace in the basement of a small Waikīkī hotel. Ducking under pipes and through a little doorway, we sat amid the array of equipment and broken machine parts that were the tools of his trade as the building's maintenance supervisor. I knew there are many martial arts practitioners from around the world who would give anything to be in the presence of this legendary man. If you saw "The Karate Kid," you'll know what I mean when I say Frank is a real-life Mr. Miyagi.

He laid back in his weathered chair, pulled out his familiar guitar, smiled and strummed as he spoke: "Don't call me master. That's a word I reserve for my teachers–the ones that have gone before us. Call me manoy, for elder. That's enough. Just manoy, okay?" Such humility was a common thread linking the contributors to this book.

These are stories that journey into the very heart of Aloha–the unique, multiethnic, cross-cultural consciousness found nowhere else on the planet. As the visionary Kenny Brown said to me one day in his comfortable office, "We're the rainbow kids, Noland. In each of our hearts beats a rhythm that makes all of us Hawaiian."

Brother Noland shares Aloha with folks at
Pālama Settlement (at right) and onstage with young
performers at the Hawai'i Theatre.

What's this book all about? Mostly, it's about how each of us might live Aloha to the fullest. Aloha is always there, of course, nestled deep within our inner spirit. Our challenge is to bring it to the surface. The magic of Aloha happens when your best and highest expression can flow naturally and honestly. It might be as simple as the look in your eyes, or as deep as the gift of unconditional love. Aloha can be acquired, discovered, learned, earned, given, shared and passed along–and that's the idea behind **The Lessons of Aloha**, a survival tool for the 21st century. To use a more Hawaiian-style metaphor, you could think of this book as a mixed plate for the spirit–saimin for the soul. It's a Hawaiian cookbook, chock-full of raw ingredients and time-tested recipes for a fuller, more rewarding life.

This volume was conceived as a book of wisdom for people of all ages. As we peer into the century ahead, of course, our thoughts naturally turn to the future generations. And so this is also very much a book for children–from small kids just beginning their journeys to older teenagers about to embark into adulthood. Read it to yourself, then read it to your child. Talk together about what you hear–and what you feel.

We all have stories to tell–stories that teach us important lessons. When I was eight, for instance, my parents split up. It was a bitter separation; they blamed one another over a relationship that may have only reached a plateau. They didn't allow each other the opportunity to discover that the only constant in life is change. And that was my first big lesson–adjusting to change in positive ways. In fact, things changed often after that. We moved from place to place. Mom worked three jobs. Dad wasn't allowed around us so, as the oldest son, I had to help out with anything and everything. Lesson No. 2: the value of helping for the greater good.

In our apartment late one night, we awoke to the sounds of forced entry. When she saw the ominous shadow of someone prying at the window, Mom let out a big scream and crawled down the hall to the room where we three kids slept. She told us not to move and we huddled together in the darkness, awaiting our fate.

After several minutes of suspense, with several very unpleasant scenarios playing in my head, I decided to take action. "We can't hide here till the sun comes up," I figured. "We should scout the enemy and prepare for battle!" That was Lesson No. 3 for me: Always trust your instincts. And Lesson No. 4: Be ready to step up to the plate when people are counting on you. I grabbed a weapon–some toy, as I recall–helped "arm" my mother, my sister Keahi and my brother Tony, and headed out to do battle. Lesson No. 5: There's safety in numbers.

Our strategy was to turn on all the lights, blast the stereo and heat up the iron as a back-up weapon! We were a nation under siege. Of course, we quickly discovered that Mom's scream had sent the burglar packing long before. It all seems pretty funny now, but as I look back on it, I realize that I began to learn something very special that night– something called survival. It was the beginning of a long and exciting journey that continues to this day.

Brother Noland, age two.

Unlike that small-kid adventure, some of the stories in this book describe events that were truly life-threatening. Others recount dark moments of the soul, or tough challenges in sports or business. Still others are uplifting tales, of good deeds done and problems met head-on. But whatever the circumstances, each of these stories is well worth a listen–for their message of Aloha, and for all they can teach us about the incredible resilience of the human spirit. ❖

Aloha,
Brother Noland

Among other youth groups, Brother Noland works closely with the kids at Palolo Elementary School.

CHAPTER ONE

The Lessons Within

If you dig deep enough, you can often find a grit and courage you didn't know was there. What does it take to recover from heroin addiction? Or to endure a hostage drama at gunpoint? How do you deal with a loved one's death at the hands of a drunk driver? Or escape the shackles of abuse, alcoholism, prostitution or physical handicap? Obviously, there's a better way to find out than going through these things yourself: just ask someone who's been there. Here are the stories of a half-dozen special folks–everyday people who ultimately found the answers deep within themselves.

James Grant Benton
Actor, Director, Playwright, Comedian

"I felt like I wen' run into one stone wall at 100 miles an hour—and that wall was addiction."

I'm not proud of these things, but I'll talk about drugs if it might help somebody. I try to make things right–make things pono. I hope others will see that I've changed–that I am a good person.

When I talk to kids, I always start with marijuana. I tell them, "Don't do it. Don't get into that." I started smoking weed in 1968–right after high school. At 19, I got the lead role in the Las Vegas production of "Hair." At that time, drugs was part of our culture. You weren't hip if you didn't do it. Marijuana made me open to trying this drug and then that drug. Each time I thought, "I can handle this." I went right up the ladder till I came to heroin. In my mind I thought I was bigger than the drugs. I learned the harsh reality years later.

We were riding the success of Booga Booga. We had money, and there were dope dealers all around. I don't blame the dealers. I take responsibility for my own actions, but when they first came on, I didn't know. They came to see the show; they socialized with you; you saw them as friends.

Then, one day Booga Booga went to do a concert on Moloka'i. My so-called friend, a drug dealer, asked me if I wanted to take some heroin with me. I said, "Nah, nah, nah, no need." We left in the morning. Our first show was at 7 that night, but by then I felt funny–really uneasy. We did the first show, but I felt terrible. Rap asked me, "What's the matter?" I said, "Brah, I don't know if I can do the second show." I was sweating and I was uncomfortable–like ants crawling under my skin. I didn't know what was wrong; I thought I had food poisoning. We canceled the rest of the shows and flew back the next

James Grant Benton's career as an actor, director, playwright and comedian has often played out on the leading edge of Hawaii's entertainment scene—from the landmark kabuki production of "Narukami the Thunder God" to his classic pidgin English adaptation of Shakespeare's "Twelfth Night" to his founding of the legendary comedy group Booga Booga with Rap Reiplinger and Ed Kaahea. He currently lends his many talents to the creative team of MBFT Media, hosts a Hawaiian radio show and gives motivational talks and training workshops to local companies and organizations.

> "You have to attack addiction with a kind of ferocity— from your heart and soul."

day. I was barfing in the bathroom at the airport and on the small Reeves airplane. I got back to Honolulu, jumped in a cab, and went straight to the hospital. I said, "Something's wrong. I think I get food poisoning." They gave me tests, but they couldn't find anything wrong, so they gave me antibiotics and said, "Go home and lie down. Maybe you get some kind of flu."

I went home and went to bed–drank chicken soup and all that. Later, my girlfriend called my so-called friend, the heroin dealer, and told him what happened. He started laughing on the phone–laughing! He said, "Come my house. He Jonesing." When she told me that, I said, "Jonesing? What's that?" He said, "Never mind, just come." I said, "No. I'm sick. I just better stay in bed for couple days." But he was very insistent. So I finally went to his apartment. There, he had heroin. Gave me a snort. Man, in about 30 seconds all that ugly feeling inside me disappeared completely. I felt like, "Wow, we go surf!" That's how quickly you get happy.

Right there I felt like I wen' run into one stone wall at 100 miles an hour–and that wall was addiction. So you start denying, but you keep going, doing the heroin. I went on for almost a year before I got caught by the police for fencing. At this point I was up to a $600-a-day habit. I was down to about 135 pounds. I was arrested, went to court, went down on 21 felony counts, and did time in jail.

It was jail time that scared me, shamed me, humbled me. The day I was going quit was just as clear as the day I realized I was hooked. From my cell window, I could see one side of the mountain–was all brown with haole koa bushes. But, had this one green tree inside of all the brown. I used that as one means of inspiring myself. I looked at that tree as if it was me. I said, "I can beat these odds." Because once you get into heroin, the odds are like 99 percent against you getting out of it. I had to start thinking of myself as the one percent. I swore out loud I was going to beat this. You have to attack addiction with that kind of ferocity–from your heart and soul.

I went to DASH (Drug Assistance Service of Hawai'i), got on methadone, and gave myself six months to get off. And, six months to the day, I got off. I wanted to get back into what I loved–acting–which was my art. At least I had that. A lot of other guys don't have anything to work towards, to look forward to.

Now, I'm an advocate. I use my acting and entertainment experience to engage kids, in hopes that they'll listen. The heroin on the street now is ten times stronger than the stuff we had. And, with "crack" and "ice," it's more of a mental addiction than physical, and mental addiction is infinitely harder to overcome than a physical addiction. Even if you get thrown into the cooler for a long time, you're not going to go through withdrawals–you no twist. It's all in your mind. You think about it–all the time. You twist mentally.

I've been trying to help my friend's son. I have to tell him straight: "It's better for your mom not to care about you, because she cannot do anything. You only making her sad. She only cry every day. I told her to cut you off already. Unless you listen, nobody will care about you."

I got him into a rehab program, but he took off. He knows I trying to help him, but he can't help himself. He gotta get to the point that he tired of hurting his family. Or, he gotta see one of his friends get killed–something that scares him enough so that he wants to quit. It's gotta start from inside, from your gut. Only then can you go through a metamorphosis and you come out of the cocoon and you one butterfly. ❖

With Rap Reiplinger and Ed Kaahea, James formed the legendary comedy group Booga Booga.

Kelly Hill

Sisters Offering Support

"Because I wanted to fit in and have friends, I was willing to compromise my own values."

I got into prostitution when I was 20 and still in university. I thought I'd do it for three months, make a lot of money in a short period of time and get out, and no one would ever know about it. But then I got caught up in it; I got greedy. And before I knew it, I had finished university and I was still doing it.

In the beginning, the money made me temporarily feel good about myself. I had no self-esteem or self-worth, of course, and I'd get a lot of attention and a certain acceptance from the customers. It was an ego boost, but it was only temporary. The next day, I'd feel so bad about what I'd done that I'd go out shopping and spend all the money just to make myself feel better again.

I was actually one of the lucky ones because at least I was an adult, not a child. I wasn't out there on the street. I was never abused. I never worked for a pimp who beat me or took my money. I was never raped or assaulted or tortured or any of those things that happen to most of our clients at SOS. But it was still completely degrading. And after a while, I began to think that I couldn't do anything else.

Even if you're not out on the street, there's nothing high-class or glamorous about prostitution. It's a woman or a young girl or child being treated like a sexual object, like a non-human, by man after man after man—men she doesn't even want to talk to, let alone have touch her intimately. There's nothing sexy or exciting about that. And I always had to leave the name and address and phone number of the person I was going out to see; then in case something happened to me and I never came back, the police would know where to look. After three years of it, I was so

*K*elly Hill's life is an open book. As the director of Sisters Offering Support, she shares her story of prostitution and recovery with the public and more important, with island girls who themselves have strayed into the world's oldest profession. When she was a young girl growing up in Canada, Kelly dreamed of becoming a television reporter. Leaving home at age 16 to work her way through school, she found a lucrative vocation in prostitution—which was legal in Canada. Since founding SOS in Honolulu in 1996, she has used her experiences to provide inspiration for many others.

> *"There's a reason for what I went through, and that's to help others."*

depressed and humiliated that I became suicidal. I'd go up to the top of my building–it was 22 stories–and think about jumping off. Either I wanted to kill the next customer I had to be with or I wanted to kill myself.

What finally turned me around was the support of my sister Christine and my grandmother Sylvia. After I finally told my sister, she never once judged me. She loved me unconditionally and helped me to believe in myself again, to motivate me and encourage me. She said, "Come on Kelly, you can do it. Go for your dreams." We started praying together and reading the Bible. We made an appointment with God every day. Just knowing that I had someone who cared about me, who loved me no matter what, finally gave me the strength to change my life.

Ever since I was little I knew I wanted to live in Hawai'i. So I moved down here to start fresh. I had two great jobs working in radio and television–what I'd always wanted–but I lost them both because I still had a lot of issues coming out of prostitution. I still couldn't work well with people at the time, especially men. Well, I was so grateful to my sister for helping me that I decided I wanted to do something to help other women get out, because it's a very isolated lifestyle and very few of them have the support they need. So I told my grandmother about what I'd done and she came down here and helped me start Sisters Offering Support.

In the beginning we wanted to help women get out of prostitution. But then we started getting calls from parents, agencies and the police department, and I became aware of all the children involved. What these kids go through really touches my heart. It's child abuse, and how they cope with it, I still cannot comprehend. I mean, I had such a hard time going through it as an adult! Our youngest client right now is 14, but I've had girls say they started as young as nine or ten. Most of them have smooth, manipulative pimps and some even have aunts and mothers in prostitution. A lot of people don't realize it because most of the young girls are not out on the streets. They're in the exotic clubs, in the hostess bars, in the massage parlors.

So how can we help them turn their lives around? At SOS, we try to offer the same kind of support that my sister gave to me. We help our clients see their options, to see all the possibilities out there, rather than just the limited perception they've had in prostitution. We have 35 volunteers now, who've been through it themselves, and this work gives them a chance to say, okay, there's a reason for what I went through, and that's to help other people. Now they're mentors and role models for our clients, providing hope, motivation and encouragement and just being there–unconditionally.

But it all goes back to when you're a kid growing up, when you're most vulnerable. When I was a teenager, I started hanging out with people who didn't share my values, who lived by different beliefs and principles. But because I wanted so desperately to fit in and have friends, I was willing to compromise my own values. My parents said, "Don't hang around with them, you'll end up the same way." I said, "No I won't." But I did. Because there's no way a kid can spend time with people with the wrong beliefs and not be influenced by them. Believe me, I know. ❖

For Kelly (right) and Christine, sisterly support started at an early age.

Tom McNeil

Contractor

"I know he didn't want to die."

From the moment I was captured, I could only think of one thing—how to escape. I've been in a couple of bad motorcycle accidents before, but that day I really thought, "This is it." My mind was racing, looking for an opportunity—but nothing came.

John Miranda wanted to kill Guy George for laying him off. He pointed the shotgun at him and blew his calf away. Guy lay there—looked like he'd bleed to death. But he managed to escape out a window, so then Miranda had one of the other hostages tape the shotgun to my neck. As we moved outside, cops were all over. SWAT dudes were dropping from a helicopter onto the roof. It was like a movie. They were still negotiating with him, but he wouldn't give up. No one knew then that he had already killed his girlfriend and was on a suicide mission.

When my friend, Kimo, saw Miranda's brother say on the news that "John's a good guy," he freaked out. He walked down the road to the TV station. On the air Kimo says, "If anyone's a good guy in this story, it's that guy with the gun to his head! He's my friend."

John was counting down from 60. He was going to kill me when he reached zero. At 13, I swung hard to my left. The shotgun came over my shoulder and went off right in my ear. "Boom!" Later the SWAT guys told me, "What you did is a textbook move. We train our guys for months to have the presence of mind to do that. Did you ever have weapons training?" I said, "No. Survival, man, survival."

Later, I got cards from all over the nation telling me, "I was praying for you all day." It really touched me. The situation was so out of control—you feel alone. When I saw Kimo, he said, "You don't have any family here who'll stick up for you." That was when I finally broke down and cried like a baby—it's so cool that people are there for you.

Still, I felt bad for John. All day, I was trying to tell him, "Man, you can live. We can all live." He chose not to. And that's so sad, because I know he didn't want to die. ❖

Tom McNeil describes moving from Canada to Hawaii in 1990 as "a dream come true." But on February 6, 1996, when Tom reported to his job at a Honolulu construction company, he became one of five hostages of a disgruntled former employee. The deadly standoff between gunman John Miranda and Honolulu police lasted for more than seven hours. As the media carried the drama live to viewers around the world, Miranda emerged from the building with a shotgun taped to Tom's neck. In a heartrending moment, he twisted free just as the shotgun fired, and Miranda was shot and killed by the police.

Kevin Daley
Drummer

"Now I call my father once a week and I say, 'You're my hero, Dad.'"

People ask me why I'm always smiling, even when things get all screwed up. I'll tell you why I smile all the time. It goes back to when I was born. I was so physically deformed that the doctors told my parents to put me in a home. I couldn't even open my hand; I was born with a fist. I was born with severe club feet. No muscles. The doctors said, "He'll never walk, he'll never do anything. Just put him in a home because he'll never be any good."

But my dad and mom said, "No, that's our kid. We're gonna do whatever we can." They took it upon themselves to give their kid a chance. They found all the best doctors in the United States. After I was a year old, when I was old enough to have operations, I was in the hospital for four years. I remember being in the hospital all the time.

My parents found the most unreal treatments. Like the guy who fixed my hands was actually a dentist. He put a little ball of plaster in my hands and said, we'll leave 'em there for a month. Then he put in bigger balls of plaster for another month, and then even bigger ones for another month, until I could keep them open.

When my father found the best orthopedic surgeon in the United States, this guy happened to be at Queen's Hospital. That's how we ended up in Hawai'i. My dad had been a hotel manager on the mainland and he went to work for Henry Kaiser to run all of his properties in Hawai'i Kai. This doctor literally cut me apart and sawed and did whatever he had to do—straighten out my legs, take a piece from here, a bone from there and throw 'em in over there.

Born in Santa Monica, California, Kevin Daley moved to Hawai'i as a *keiki* and grew up along with the fledgling community of Hawai'i Kai. "Lunalilo Home Road was just a dusty road leading through the pig farms on the way to Sandy Beach," he recalls. "As a JPO holding a stop sign in front of Koko Head Elementary, I had to eat that dust every day after school!" Kevin went on to become a journeyman drummer with various O'ahu bands and is today married to Christine Mendoza Daley, a vocalist and a percussionist in her own right.

> "What's so cool was the people who first embraced me were the Hawaiians."

Back then, Hawai'i Kai was a place with huge empty open spaces divided by the marinas. It was a kid's dream, for riding bikes, swimming, surfing, hiking, playing barefoot football and anything else you could think of. Then when I started hanging around with surfers, the surfing began to make my back strong.

What's so cool was the people who first embraced me were the Hawaiians. It was the local Hawaiian people who took an interest in me. Like, wow, look at this skinny, haole white dude, but he get this energy, you know. I was five or six years old, just hanging around with all local guys. Nobody treated me different. It was a total blessing. I call it the Hawaiian thing. It's like, you're normal, you cool, let's just go, brah. Come on. Jump in the car. Let's go surf. It's totally Hawaiian. So I grew up surfing with guys like Reno Abellira and later Michael and Derek Ho in Waimānalo. Of course, I didn't know these guys were going to be big surfing stars someday. They would take me out and because they knew all the guys, they would tell everybody else, "Don't catch this wave!" And they'd tell me, "Okay, go!" They would let me catch the waves and that's how I got into it.

Later I met Randy Lorenzo and Mackey Feary and all those guys in high school, and I started to play drums. And then all of a sudden I'm this skinny haole guy playing with Gabby Pahinui. Everybody's saying, who's this guy playing drums with Gabby? Well, just from hanging around with people who didn't think I was handicapped changed my whole attitude—literally put it out of my head. I just loved life because, hey, I'm hanging out with the guys and I'm surfing and I'm playing music.

As I got older, of course, there were drugs around, and I screwed up. Went through a real hard time—lost my first wife, lost my livelihood, homeless, living in a junky car. The only thing I still had was my drums. Why? Like Earth, Wind & Fire was gonna call me for a gig? But something told me my drums were important for the future.

By this time, my dad was senior vice president at First Hawaiian Bank. But what was cool was that he didn't give me money then. He said you have to learn to live life on your own. Still, they never gave up on me, and they helped me get over the hard times in other ways.

To this day, my father and my mom, Don and Gloria Daley, are my guardian angels. They're retired in Virginia now and loving life. Two years ago, my dad called me and said, "Guess what?"

"What?"

"You're mine, you're finally mine."

I said, "What are you talking about?"

"You're finally mine! I just paid the last of all those doctor's bills from when you were a kid."

I had chicken skin. I was overwhelmed. It turns out, my whole life, even when I was screwing up on drugs or whatever, he was paying my doctor bills. Here I'm 46 years old. My dad is 86 years old. And he finally paid it all off two years ago.

My dad is my idol. Now I call my father once a week and I say, "You're my hero, Dad."

And now you know why I'm always smiling. ❖

Kevin attacks the drums at an Aloha Stadium rock concert.

Donna Tyler
Mothers Against Drunk Driving

"Why should these youngsters learn from tragedy, when they can learn from someone else?"

I remember that evening vividly because my brother and his best friend were really excited about attending their first junior high dance. I was a senior in high school, and my attitude was, "Leave me alone. Big deal." At that time I didn't want anything to do with my little brother. I had my own things to do.

That evening, I went to the movies with my friends and I came home around 11:30 at night. There were all these lights on in the house, which was peculiar, and unfamiliar cars parked out front. I walked in the house and my father tells me, "Donna, your brother's been in a fatal crash." Well, "fatal" just didn't register, you know, he's a 14-year-old. Fatal. My father repeated, "Donna, your brother has died in a car crash." My reaction was complete shock. I just couldn't believe it.

He and his friend were walking along the side of the road and this 17-year-old driver was coming home from a party with her girlfriends. She hit my brother. He died instantly. She dragged his best friend down the road and he died a week later.

When this opportunity came up to work for MADD, it just felt right. I feel like I'm supposed to be doing this for our community. I go to the high schools and share my story about my brother. It's not easy to talk about losing a brother, but my role is to try to prevent it, you know. Why should these youngsters learn from tragedy, when they can learn from someone else? Kids come up and thank me for sharing my stories. They even send letters and cards thanking me. I'm hoping I'm making a difference.

You know what I learned from this? That you can't take life for granted and your loved ones for granted. You don't know. They may not be around tomorrow because death is final—you don't have a second chance. This tragedy brought our family closer together. But why should you love your parents or show them more affection after your brother dies? I mean, you should be doing it now. ❖

At first glance, you might guess that Donna Tyler is a model, a sales rep or a beauty consultant—all of which she has been. Not satisfied with her career goals, however, Donna responded to an ad in the newspaper for a youth coordinator for MADD (Mothers Against Drunk Driving). After two years on the job, she says, "I feel like I've found my calling. I love working with kids." The strength of Donna's conviction comes from the personal loss of her own brother in a drunk driving accident. Today she has two children of her own—Arianna (opposite, left) and Chloe.

Nancy Ishimoto and Shawn

"You are one of many and you're no more special than anybody else."

Everything was fine–a normal pregnancy–and he was born a happy, smiley baby. Always. Never failed. Then, when he was five weeks old, the doctors discovered he had a very rare cancer in his eyes. The ophthalmologist said, "It's not a matter of saving his sight, it's a matter of saving his life." They had to remove both of his eyes.

There are no books on how to raise a blind kid, so I figured, we'll just raise a child. We're all handicapped in our own way, right? You love them, no matter what. The hugging and the kissing–that should not stop. You don't reach a certain age and go, "Whoa, I'm too big for that." I still hug and kiss my parents. When you're feeling rotten, you can go give someone a hug and you feel good inside.

We didn't coddle him, though. We always wanted him to be independent. We fought with his teachers at school who tried to segregate the kids and say, "Oh you're special." I kept saying, "No. You're no more special than the next person. I'm sorry, but the world is not centered around you. You're a part of a unit, a family unit, which is a part of a bigger unit, which is your community, which is a part of a bigger unit–which is society, Hawai'i. You are one of many and you're no more special than anybody else."

I'd see what little homework he would be given to do, and I would go and meet with the teachers. I'd say, "I don't want a 'B' for blind; I don't want a 'C' for cute. I want real grades. If he's flunking, tell him he's flunking. Don't pass him from grade to grade just because you feel sorry for him." I said, "Who are you helping here? How much work is he going to have in

Blind since he was but a few weeks old, Shawn demonstrated an amazing affinity for music from a very young age—playing bass, guitar, ukulele and drums. His guitar playing began to attract the public's attention when he was still in high school. Turning professional in 1996, he already has two successful recording projects under his belt and more in the works. Managed by his mother, Nancy Ishimoto, Shawn has also established his own record label and publishing company called Flying Solo and is producing the works of other young artists.

society when he grows up and tries to find a job? He's going to end up being dependent on the state to support him."

One very important valuable part of the training he received in IEP (Individual Educational Program) was how to catch the bus. He would walk from our house in Foster Village to the main street where the bus stop is. He'd take a bus over to Pearlridge, then transfer to a bus up to 'Aiea High School. They'd drop him off and he'd walk the rest of the way.

He's a very trusting person and hardly had problems figuring things out. There were a number of times when the bus driver would forget his stop, however. Sometimes he'd end up down in Waikīkī, or Waipahu side, and he wouldn't know where he was. He's good about it, though. He doesn't let it faze him. He doesn't mind asking somebody, "Excuse me, where are we and what bus do I need to catch to go somewhere?" He always got to where he needed to go. He's very independent.

Later, we got him a cell phone in case he had a problem finding his way. When he was late, I scolded him, "We were worried. Why didn't you call? You should call if you're going to be home after dark." He'd laugh and say, "Mom, it's always dark!"

That's the kind of spirit he has. You gotta find humor in everything, you gotta learn to laugh at yourself. We've learned that what you have is what you have—you live with it, you deal with it, and you move on. ❖

Rather than raise a blind child,
Nancy chose to "just raise a child."

CHAPTER TWO

Lessons in the Community

Everyone feels
isolated–even abandoned–once in a while.
The good news is that there's always someone
out there for us at times like this: community
servants who know the true meaning of
sacrifice–and who will never abandon you.
Some are paid for their services; many more
volunteer selflessly. But sometimes, the hardest
part is reaching out to these helpers and healers.
"We will give more than you thought anyone
could give," they tell us, "but you must
be there to accept it. Don't be afraid to
ask for help–for yourself or your loved ones.
Meet us halfway with your positive
energy, for that is the only way
this can really work."

Mary Scott Lau
Women In Need

"They already know about dying.
They want me to teach them how to live."

I n the beginning I wasn't even sure I could do this. I volunteered for counseling at the Spouse Abuse Shelter, but on the very first night I was in their office crying. There were some really bad cases in there, including a little girl who was being abused by her father. This girl zeroed right in on me. She came over and sat on my lap the whole time I was teaching. And I knew during the class that her father was coming to take her back. I just couldn't control it. I was trying to teach something, but my heart was breaking. So I went into the office and I said, "I can't do this. It's just too painful." But the director said, "You have to. They need you too much." So I went back and after awhile, those classes got a little easier. I mean, I still cry in class, but now I realize that if it's hard for me, it's all been a lot harder for them.

When I work with the AIDS and HIV-positive groups, these girls don't want to talk about their HIV. They already know about dying. Instead, they want to have fun. They want to live, and they want me to teach them how to live. I remember one girl, about 15 years old, she's carrying this book.

I say, "What are you reading?"

"Oh," she says, "it tells you how to end your life gracefully."

I couldn't believe it. "You're thinking of killing yourself?"

And she goes, "I'm tired of the pain."

Well, that day we had a great time in class, learning about makeup and facials, and afterwards she says, "That was really fun!"

M ainland transplant Mary Scott Lau has made Hawai'i home for over 20 years. After stints in advertising, marketing, television news and modeling, Mary founded the support group Women In Need. As WIN's executive director, she teaches classes in basic life skills—personal hygiene, wardrobe planning, family finances and much more—at the Mary Jane Center (for girls and women with unplanned pregnancies), Hale Kipa, the Institute for Human Services, the Women's Addiction Treatment Center of Hawai'i and other agencies. In her "spare" time, she writes grant proposals, raises her three sons and teaches Sunday school!

24

So I say, "Will you do me a favor? Will you put that book away for a week, until next Tuesday's class?" She said yeah, and we did the same thing the next week, and then she's coming every week. Sometimes she's great and sometimes she's sick and sometimes she's even high. But at least she comes. 'Cause it doesn't matter how they get there, just that they get there. And we have a ball.

One day, one of the girls at the Mary Jane Center called me up crying. She said, "My mother just got arrested and they're sending her to prison!" It turns out this woman had skipped probation on a felony charge in Arizona. So I went down and calmed her down, and then I called an emergency class.

I said, "The name of this class is 'bad mothers.' And I know what I'm talking about, because I'm a survivor child just like you."

You see, my mother was an alcoholic, and my brother and I were taken away from her when I was ten and he was six. She absolutely adored us, but she had this bad drinking problem and she'd leave us alone. I used to pray to God for her to stop drinking and stop running away. My brother and I were illegitimate, we didn't know our fathers, so our godmother took us in. About six years later, my mother got pretty crazy–started trying to commit suicide. When I was 20 she finally succeeded. When I turned 21 they gave me custody of my brother. And not too long ago, my brother died of a heroin overdose at age 37, after 20 years of trying to lead a clean and sober life.

So I never had that role model. My mother wasn't what I wanted her to be. But I'll tell you what–I'm a great mother myself. And I challenged the girls in that class to be the same kind of fabulous mother. I said, "I'm sorry you have bad mothers. I cry for you the way I cried for me. But you can break the cycle." Nobody talked. They just sat there and

> "I'm sorry you have bad mothers. But you can break the cycle."

cried, and I hugged them all. To this day, if you ask them what their favorite class was, they'll say "bad mothers."

You know, a funny thing happened after my brother died. I had expected it for so long, because he struggled with drugs for years. So I didn't cry in any of my classes, even though it was always on my mind. But my students cried because they all knew about my brother and how I had tried to help him. And then one day in class, I was trying to get the message across about not doing drugs, and I just started crying and I couldn't stop. I was so embarrassed, but the kids were just ecstatic that I was sharing with them like that. They were feeling somehow privileged that I broke down in front of them. The whole class was around me, supporting me. What a great way to get my message across!

We all need a support system. Sometimes you just can't make it on your own. It's the 'ohana concept, big-time. As long as they feel they have someone who will support them and care about them, anyone can make it. Nobody escapes the bad times in life. But it's what you do with them that counts. What you learn from them. And how you help other people learn, too. ❖

At the Mary Jane Center, Mary helps new mothers find new beginnings.

Chauncey Pang
Word of Life Christian Center

"Being around haoles, blacks, Hispanics and others, I began to appreciate life more."

My family was very, very close, and there was a lot of love and aloha in our home. We was raised to always take care of one another—malama each other, you know. You look out for the interest of other people. Even if it's your last dime, you do whatever it takes to make sure that if that person need money for catch the bus to get home, you give that person the money. If I gotta walk up the heights, I'll walk up the heights.

I was raised up in Papakōlea. I went to Pauoa Elementary, then Stevenson Intermediate. When my dad came back from Vietnam, he got stationed at Schofield Barracks, so our family had to move. I really didn't want to move because I felt I cannot handle being around haoles. My mentality was they came here and stole my heritage, so I had a bad perspective of them. I bucked heads with Mommy and Dad. I said, "Why don't Daddy go there? We go stay here with Auntie them. We go there and stay on the weekends. But, of course, we couldn't. Anyway, we moved to Schofield Barracks. I finished up part of my intermediate years and my high school years at Leilehua.

Living in Schofield Barracks taught me a lot. It opened up my eyes to see that there's a lot of good people. I was so limited. All I wanted to do was be around local people and I didn't want to include anybody else in my world.

Being down there brought me out of my box and helped to build character in me. I began to see that there's a lot of things that these other nationalities had that I didn't have. And I began to see things of value to

Chauncey Pang was born in 1957 in Colorado, where his father, a career Army sergeant, was stationed. Upon retiring, his Hawai'i-born parents decided to move home to the Islands—settling first in Papakōlea before moving to Schofield Barracks. In 1980, he got married and moved to North Carolina. In 1984, he returned to Hawai'i with his family. Chauncey has been associated with the Word of Life Christian Center for 12 years—as a full-time pastor for the past five. "Before I came here, my life had a lot of ups and downs," he says. He now uses the lessons he learned through his personal experience and hardships to help people in need.

> **"I cannot turn my back on these people who have reached out to me."**

them that helped me to see areas of weakness in my life. I could better appreciate all the different nationalities.

Being around a lot of haole people, black people, Hispanic people and others, I began to appreciate life more. I learned that the true aloha spirit was to love everybody.

I remember one year when I was in high school, they had this day called "Kill Haole Day." The boys there said, "Come on Chaunce, today's the big day, man." So everybody was set to really take it to the hoop, but I didn't want to get involved in it.

I valued the relationships with a lot of the haole people and blacks and the others. I said, "No, I can't do it. I cannot turn my back on these people who have reached out to me, invited me into their homes, shared their life with me." I said to myself, "I don't care if the local people turn against me." And some of my friends did. They called me a coward and stuff, but I didn't care.

These people that came from the mainland, they didn't understand. "What is 'Kill Haole Day,' Chaunce? What did I do?" Some of my friends are getting cracked in front of the library, you know, some of them are just getting pushed for no reason, so I stood up for some of these people. They stayed by me and these other local guys would back off because they saw that I was ready to stand up for them.

I tried to help them understand that it was just a thing that we grew up with, you know. I had to explain to them that I wasn't like that. I said, "I want you to know that I am Hawaiian, I'm local. I want you to know that you're my friends, man. And I love and I appreciate you guys." Through that I developed some great relationships. But the most important thing that I've learned was the value of appreciating people—appreciating life. Because there's something good in everybody.

Funny thing is, a few years later I got a taste of what racism can really be like. I moved to Florida for six or seven months when I was building cable systems throughout the southern states. I was living down in Coral Gables right after the Liberty City riots between the blacks and the police. Not to mention all the drug transactions: heavy, heavy vibes. Plenty hatred and extreme violence. They found a body in the trunk of a car at the motel where I was staying. Plus, Castro was letting a lot of people go and the flotillas were coming in from Cuba. All us local guys could pass for Cubans, you know. And when I had to pull cable through people's back yards, they thought I was Cuban and they used to treat me real mean. So now I was feeling what it's like to be on the receiving end of racism.

When I think back to my high school days, I realize that being around other kinds of people helped to bring the best out of me. Before, I had really been limiting myself. When I opened myself up, it brought things out in me that I thought I would never be able to share. So I gained a lot from it and I've tried to carry that throughout my life. ❖

Chauncey learned the lessons of ethnic diversity as a young man.

Kamani Kualaau
Kamehameha Schools Alumnus

"You can't worry about the consequences if you believe what you're doing is right."

I happened to get involved with student government by luck or fate—whatever you want to call it. I had no interest in student government until I entered the ninth grade, when my counselor asked me if I was interested in running for class office. I said okay and put in the application—and that's how I got started.

I enjoyed planning functions for my classmates—making them happy. I came to value their trust. When they brought something to my attention or asked me a question, I would write it down, go find the answers and get back to them. It felt good to be able to help. And I also developed a deep love and respect for Kamehameha Schools in the process.

Being involved in student government I got to converse with classmates, teachers, administrators—everybody. Thus, as we approached graduation, it became clear that something wasn't right at the school. Knowing that things weren't pono at Kamehameha, we felt that we had to at least try to set things straight. The senior class president and I sat down and wrote a letter to the trustees telling them that something ought to be done to address the situation.

The letter was meant to be positive—nothing negative. We didn't want to slam anyone or anything in particular. We wrote the letter on behalf of the students, but we were the ones to sign our names on it. Someone had to be accountable, so we put our names out there, saying, "This is what we think." And we were prepared to take whatever flak came from it.

We were just doing what we thought we had to do. It seemed like the logical step to take. When the alumni realized that the school—the students in particular—was being affected, that was all it took. That's when they all got together.

Through it all, I never doubted what we were doing. We weren't worried. In that sense it was easy. It felt natural. You can't worry about what the consequences are going to be if you believe what you're doing is the right thing to do. ❖

Kamani Kualaau is in his third year at Princeton University. As student body president of Kamehameha Schools in 1997, he collaborated with a friend to write a letter to the school's board of trustees, telling them that something was amiss at Kamehameha. That letter set into motion a remarkable series of transformative events—with repercussions throughout the community. Today, Kamani's still-youthful world continues to expand. "There is a much broader community out there," he notes. "How can we all work together toward the greater good? Not only Hawaiians, but people in general."

Martha Sanchez
Mercado de la Raza

"You see how expensive Hawai'i is? But to me it's a price I'm willing to pay for peace of mind."

Sometimes my kids start thinking, "Why can't we have this?" or, "I wish we had that." So I tell them every morning, "When you get up every day, you count your blessings, not your miseries. Every morning you get up and say, "Wow, look, the sun came up. My mom has cereal for me, and milk, you know. Be grateful that you're alive, and that you're fortunate enough to live in Hawai'i."

I lived on the mainland, so I know what it's like to go to a store and they tell you, "Oh, you Mexican," and make derogatory statements. Here, you can go into any store—fancy store—dressed as you are, and no one is going to send for security. If I go Beverly Hills dressed like this? Forget it! You want to buy a house? They told me, "We show you where we think you'll be more comfortable." "Well, I'm not comfortable there. I want to buy the house over there." "No, but I don't think you'll be happy there."

Living in Hawai'i has given me a chance to grow because I don't have the extra burden of having to worry about being discriminated against. Because of the diversity here, it doesn't matter what we look like, right? If I open my mouth, you can hear my accent, but if you see me walking down the street you're going to think I'm local, right?

When you have kids, you stop thinking about yourself and only think about your kids. Here, I don't have to worry if my kids going get beat up or be called names in school. You don't have to fear that somebody's going to shoot at you, or tell you to go back to where you came from. So I tell my kids, "You see how expensive Hawai'i is? But to me peace of mind has a price. It's a price I'm willing to pay for peace of mind."

Martha Sanchez owns and operates Mercado de la Raza, a Hispanic grocery store on Beretania Street, and a second store in Wahiawa. Her stores serve as meeting places for Hawaii's Hispanic community. In addition to importing favorite foods, Martha also gives cooking lessons, works with schools who wish to arrange excursions to her store, and gives talks to groups that want to learn more about Hispanic culture. Her efforts helped to inspire the opening of the nonprofit Hispanic Center of Hawai'i. The center serves as a gathering place that also provides translation, notary and referral services.

34

> *"I tell my kids,
> 'You are
> Hawaiian—maybe
> not by blood,
> but by birth you
> are Hawaiian.'"*

On the other hand, I feel like I should send my kids to school on the mainland, because I want them to learn to survive. I know that it's a real awakening when you go to the mainland. It's scary. Over here, it's so secure that sometimes I think we're too comfortable. To me, my kids don't have the edge to compete on the mainland. I opened my business because I'm hungry. I want to survive. I don't want to go back to the mainland where I was verbally abused; you know, it almost killed me spiritually.

Whenever I felt myself alone, backed up against a wall, I remembered what my father would always say in Spanish: "It's better to die on your feet than on your knees." And I always used to think that. I used to say that out loud. That really kept me going.

Here in Hawai'i, many of your parents and grandparents worked hard on the plantation, and they didn't want their kids to have to work as hard as they did, so they want their kids to go to private school, college. But those kids forgot about the hardships of the past; they don't know about it. They don't appreciate what they have because they have never suffered.

It should be a requirement to work before you graduate from high school. That's why I tell my kids, "Go help somebody. Go volunteer at Pālama Settlement. Be an orderly in a hospital before you go to the mainland, because I want you to see suffering, I want you to see pain. You have more than many others. They don't have an idea. When something doesn't cost you anything, you don't take care of it.

My father would often say, "Maybe nobody is indispensable in this world, but you can still make yourself indispensable." I tell my kids, "Don't ask, 'Do you have a job for me?' or, 'Do you need help?' Everybody needs help. You ask, 'Do you have a broom? I can help you sweep up over here.' Roll up your sleeves and start cleaning, or start lifting boxes—whatever needs to be done. You always go and make yourself useful." And that has always been my philosophy whenever I go to any job.

My two kids are half Mexican and half Korean, but I tell them they're Hawaiian. My former husband says, "No. Don't tell them that." But I tell my kids, "You are Hawaiian—maybe not by blood, but by birth you are Hawaiian." I believe if you don't realize that you're Hawaiian, you're not going to take care of the land the same way that a Hawaiian would care of it. When you truly love where you were born, you'll take care of it.

I taught my kids to recycle from when they were very young, and I explained to them why. "You are responsible for these mountains. You are responsible for people who throw oil or garbage down the stream, because we all bathe in it, we swim in it, we drink it." I say, "When you have kids, there's not going to be room. The beaches going be full of garbage and you won't be able to enjoy the beaches." We are the ones who are going to pass on the culture to the following generations.

Living here in Hawai'i for 22 years, it kind of made me sad to hear the degree of ignorance about Hispanics, because we are such a small group here, such a minority. It bothers me to hear people asking the same questions. I don't mind the jokes, because to me we have to laugh at ourselves. That's very Mexican; Mexican humor is really sarcastic, but there has to be enough knowledge about the culture so that there is that respect, too, you know. That's adding to Hawaii's diversity.

I opened a store because I wanted to sell the things that share my culture. I open it up to schools and I give talks to school children, because prejudice is a learned thing. If we will take the time to see the similarities in all different cultures instead of our differences, it'll be easier for us to get along. ❖

Martha's father Merced Sanchez Tapia: "You can make yourself indispensable."

Verna Keyes
Pālama Settlement

"Owning things doesn't make you a better person."

My father worked at Pearl Harbor and my mother at a lei stand down the old airport. We didn't have very much, but we didn't think we were deprived. It was just part of life. You had to make a living, so you worked, you went to school, you did your best–that's how it was.

My father was real hands-on. He felt that by actually doing something and showing you, it would stick with you more than just telling you. When I was a young kid growing up down by Damon Tract, there was a lot of kiawe trees all over down there. We would spread 18 Coleman lanterns all over underneath those trees, so that all the lei sellers would have light to work by each night. In the morning, as soon as the sun came up, my father would say, "Okay, it's time to bring in the lanterns." And he himself would go help me pick up all the lanterns and bring them in and shut them off.

In the afternoon, we had to fill the lanterns, change all the mantles and pump them up to make sure they wouldn't go out. Many times when the Coleman lanterns would die, my mother would give us dirty lickings because we allowed it to go out. But not my father. If he saw the lantern flickering, he would go over there, take the lantern off the tree, and pump like crazy so the lantern would be bright.

My dad was Chinese–Hakka, the farmers of China. And he was a very hard worker, and very into family. He believed very strongly in the importance of education. His whole thing was you sacrifice on behalf of the kids so that the next generation will

> Verna Keyes was born in Honolulu to a Chinese father who was the oldest of 12 children and a Hawaiian mother from rural Maui. After studying at Honolulu Business College and the National School of Aeronautics in Kansas City, Verna started her work at Pālama Settlement more than 20 years ago. Today she is the director of Community and Neighborhood Development there. She also studies and practices lomilomi with kupuna Margaret Machado, a master of the art of healing massage. "Healing people in this way," she says, "makes me feel I am truly doing the Lord's work."

38

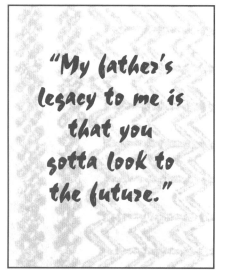

"My father's legacy to me is that you gotta look to the future."

become better and carry your name. My father was very insistent that the family name be kept clean. It was very, very important to him.

My mother passed on at least 20 years before my father. My father felt very firm that he would do anything so that his family would have a better life than him. And so as a result he left the house to me.

But then, a few years ago, I could see the handwriting on the wall: financially I wasn't equipped to keep the house. I went into the candy vending business to help bring in extra revenue–to try to keep up with the house expenses. I had to go all over–fill the candy machines and whatever. It was hard work. My daughter and my grandkids thought, "Oh, grandma is super lady. There's no big worry." I tried many different ways to show them that I have the strength and energy to make it work, but I need the support. I cannot do it by myself.

By the early part of last year, I had to look at things in a matter-of-fact way. My attorney kept telling me, "You know, you're gonna be going downhill and what's going to happen after that?" So I went to the grave to talk to my father to tell him, "You know what, Daddy? I'm having a real hard time. And I know, spiritually, you know that I am. So you either gotta send me more help, or I gotta go take the course that I gotta take."

My father's legacy to me is to know that you gotta look to the future–the future being in the kids–and the kids is your family, whatever the family is. To him, whatever it is you're trying to do, you must have your kids' best interest at heart.

Well, it took me another six to eight months to let go of the house, because I tied the house to my dad. There was a lot of inner conflict, but I have a very deep spiritual sense. Spiritual stuff, if you have it inside, and if you really build on it, and if you truly believe, then nobody else can steal that from you. Nobody. And I know that even if we want to hang on to our material things, they can be taken from you. I remember my father and my mother always saying that, and I think that is what carried me through this decision.

It was very difficult, but I was determined that I was not going to be destitute. I was determined that this was not going to bring me down. Everything that my father and mother did for me was for a reason.

I had to look inside myself and say, "Okay, so I'm not going to have something tangible for my grandkids. But in all these years that I raised all five of them, if I have not taught them the essence of what living really is, then the house means absolutely nothing. And for those who will think less of you because you no longer own this, that's fine too. Those that really care for you will be with you no matter what. Owning things doesn't make you a better person."

You know, letting go of that house has brought me so many other positive things since then. And that's the only way to look at life—being very, very positive. ❖

Verna's father, Alfred Chung, (here with a young lei seller) taught his children traditional Chinese family values.

Ken Yamamoto

Educator

"All geniuses express or design.
Look at Leonardo da Vinci, Thomas Edison—
all geniuses create."

There have been a lot of studies done recently on how geniuses think. One finding is that all geniuses express or design. Look at Leonardo da Vinci, Thomas Edison–all geniuses create. So when you teach kids, have them do something: act it out, draw it out, make an ukulele, play a song, whatever. Then they'll connect things that aren't connected, and then they'll see metaphors. It isn't hard to do, but we don't seem to place an importance on it, so people don't do it.

Research has also shown that creativity exists naturally in young children, but dies out at about the fourth or fifth grade–and thereafter it's gone. Schools, which have to enforce discipline and order, are partly responsible, but it's also due to the parents' value systems. Also, up to that point, kids are intuitive, natural. About age eight, they start reasoning, thinking logically.

So, to me, the kid better be loved and know what love is by age eight. They have to experience giving love to others–and not just verbally. I've seen parents tell their kids, "I love you" all the time. They mean it, but it still doesn't work, because the kid has not done it. You have to help them help people. Say you go to Ala Moana Center, and an old person falls down–take your kid, grab the person's hand and help them. They have to do that or they will never understand what love is.

The child has to learn that life's a journey. They gotta learn that they have choices. They gotta learn what love is, how to express love, and that you don't wait for love. It has to be inside you already, and that you use it.

Ken Yamamoto recently retired from the Department of Education (DOE). He served as assistant superintendent for curriculum, where he was in charge of all instruction, evaluation and teacher training. Ken has always been an educator. Besides his teaching career with the DOE, he also ran his own private business, offering tutorial services after school and on Saturdays, working with surrogate parents, disabled children and high school drop-outs. Ken is also a student and practitioner of Asian spiritual arts and offers his services as a consultant to individuals and businesses.

When you look at kids' art, it's beautiful–the colors are vibrant, you know. I can tell kids, "Here's a crayon and pencil; go draw." And they will. But music seems to scare people. They don't seem to understand it. They think it's an inherent talent.

I tell teachers, "Just do Bacon, Lettuce, Tomato every day." When they go, "What?" I say, "BLT: Beauty, Love, Truth." I encourage them to have the kids sing in the classroom every day. It doesn't matter what. Everything is beautiful. You need to eliminate ugly.

It's polarities, yin and yang. Until you experience both sides, you have no depth. The more you experience polarities, the better you'll understand. For example, you might see something and say, "Wow, that's beautiful." But if I tell you, "Define beauty"–nobody can. They go, "Beauty? Well, it's nice." Then I say, "Well, beauty is not just 'nice.' Do you like cow dung? Eh, to the dung beetle, cow dung is beautiful." Everything has a purpose, everything has a reason, everything has a consequence.

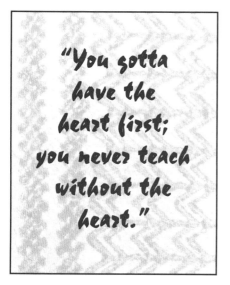

"You gotta have the heart first; you never teach without the heart."

So when you see ugly, don't get upset. Because now things that people think are ugly, you can say, "Okay, I can see the other side of the coin." So there's no ugly anymore. You create a different world when you see beauty. That's how life is made more meaningful.

But people don't think like that. For many, life is meaningless. It's chaos. And they wonder, "Why me?" Or, "Why is this happening?" Everything has a purpose. Sometimes we cannot know everything, but at least we should have a means of saying, "Okay, right now I don't know why this is happening to me, but one day I'll know."

That's why the Bacon, Lettuce, Tomato is so powerful, because there's magic when you appreciate beauty. The love naturally flows out, and when that happens, then you can see the truth. You gotta have the heart first; you never teach without the heart. If not, once the kid's logic kicks in, the logic moves toward the technical–to build better bombs, perhaps. If you teach only from the brain, then kids will learn cold facts. They have to have a whole sense of love already, so when they deal with the facts, they'll use those facts for good. I still always tell people, "The bottom line, folks, is love. And you guys are scared of it. But if you don't help the kids do that, it's all worthless." ❖

CHAPTER THREE

Lessons of the Land

Island people
need to be outdoors. It's one big reason
they live in Hawai'i in the first place.
They're physical people–in tune with nature,
respecting it, trusting it. Out in the country–
on a lonely stretch of beach or a misty mountain
laced with waterfalls–the world is magnified,
the wind sings, the colors come alive.
Fresh from the big city, it might even take you
awhile to get in sync, to catch your breath.
But then you feel the energy of the earth beneath
your feet; you get the rhythm back. For the
islanders who share their thoughts on these pages,
that rhythm comes naturally, for these are people
who make their living or gather their sustenance
or learn their lessons from the 'āina.

Walter Ritte, Jr.
Farmer and Hawaiian Visionary

"The kūpuna always made sure we knew what was right and what was wrong."

WALTER RITTE, JR.

The first march we ever did was when the people of Moloka'i marched against Moloka'i Ranch. On Moloka'i, the ranch is the mighty man on the great white horse. If you like go fishing, then you gotta have good standing with the ranch. You like go hunting, you gotta have good standing with the ranch. The ranch was the most powerful entity on the island.

So when we went to march against them, it was like the first time in the history of Moloka'i where people was actually going to do something against the ranch. We expected 25 guys, 30 guys. Well, 200 guys wen' show up for march—and this was the days when marching wasn't one fad. The ranchers waited on the hill with the game wardens and police, ready for arrest anybody who came on the property. It became a confrontation. Everybody was scared to death. We felt brave because get 200 guys—the ranch had only about 20 guys on the hill. We knew they couldn't stop us.

We made this fence the issue, because we knew that private property ended at the high water mark, so their fence was on public property—was illegal. So we said, "They got no business having a fence there."

So we go over there and knock down the fence. Down goes the fence. Everybody marching through. We was the last guys in the back and the kūpuna said, "Now you guys gotta put the fence back up."

Of course we said, "No! It's a matter of principle. The fence is illegal. We have every right to knock down the fence, and they can never put it back up again!"

A taro farmer on the island of Moloka'i—where he lives with his wife, Loretta, and his children and grandchildren—Walter Ritte, Jr., first made headlines in the 1970s as a vocal Hawaiian rights activist. Spearheading the Protect Kaho'olawe 'Ohana and other grassroots groups, the Rittes and their friends and associates challenged beach access restrictions on Moloka'i and U.S. Navy target practice on Kaho'olawe, among other issues. On Kaho'olawe, they sowed native plants and restored historical sites, even as they worked to stop the bombing and increase public awareness of aloha 'āina—love of the land.

But the kūpuna argued that all the cows from the ranch goin' get mixed up with the cows from the Hawaiian homestead. It was a matter of common sense. Even though we was making our points known, right is right and wrong is wrong. The reality of the whole thing was that uncle them, who work for the ranch, goin' have to spend two weeks sorting out cows.

"You like uncle them go through all that?" the kūpuna said. "You proved your stuff, now get back to your life."

So, after everybody went we put the fence back up. It was hard, because I never like put back the fence. The fence is illegal, but that wasn't all there was to that. The real life part was why the fence was there in the first place. That was the role the kūpuna played. They always made sure we knew what was right and what was wrong. That was the key.

They didn't teach Hawaiian stuff in high school or the university back when we was going to school. You had to go learn 'em. You had to go do 'em. Knowledge wasn't from books. Mainly, the knowledge came from the kūpuna. We had this connection with the kūpuna because without that we no had nothing. That was what made us really strong.

The stuff we was learning made us angry. All the bad things that they did to Hawaiians: the overthrow of Queen Lili'uokalani, how out of one million Hawaiians the population was way down to 40,000, about the land that was stolen.

During a 1970s march on Moloka'i, a bullhorn-wielding Walter is counseled by a kupuna.

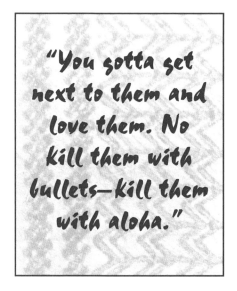

"You gotta get next to them and love them. No kill them with bullets—kill them with aloha."

With all this negative stuff coming out, Kaho'olawe was the thing that jelled everything together. And the jelling point was simple—the jelling point was love. We found out you cannot win against the United States military on their own terms. The only way you can win is to love them. And yet we hated them for what they was doing. So how can we love them? That's the kind of controversial stuff we were trying to learn in life. In the end, we learned you gotta beat them by loving them. You gotta get right next to them and you gotta love them. No kill them with bullets–kill them with aloha.

At Kaho'olawe we learned there is nothing more powerful than love. Hate just cannot compare to it. Nothing can compare to it. And that's what the kūpuna had been telling us.

Yeah, I know I made lot of enemies–bankers, developers, like that. But I tell them we have to look ahead. If I really care about my kids, then I gotta look seven generations down the road. That's how I think. Will it be good for them? If you don't look that far ahead, then the limited resources you have going be gone.

It's like the fishponds over here on Moloka'i. Unreal–the walls are 800 years old and still strong. And you know why? Not because they just build 'em and the water never go bust the wall. Of course the water goin' bust 'em, all the time, but then they went and put it back. That's another thing we learned. You cannot just leave your resources alone. You gotta keep going back and working on 'em–even if it's for 800 years! ❖

Moku Buchanan
Family Man

"Life is precious, so you gotta make use of it every day."

My grandparents adopted me when I was three years old because my mother and father got divorced. I've always called my grandparents "Mom" and "Dad." They raised me the best they could, with lots of love, and taught me a lot of values.

The toughest thing for me was when Mom died. She was suffering from cancer and I was with her every day at the hospital. It got to the point where we knew she wasn't going to get better, and I started coming weak. I was to the point where I wanted her to die already, because I love her so much that I no like her suffer anymore. So I ask God, "How come you doing this to this lady? She's such a nice and loving lady. All she did her whole life was give. Why you letting her suffer like this?"

I was kinda getting mad. I guess that's just human–lots of different emotions going on inside of you. I went home that evening and my dad called and said right after I left my mom died. I cried because I was sad that she left, but yet was tears of joy, too. It was like God wen' show me: "No worry, boy, I'm in control. She's home with me and she's fine."

At first, I was thinking I no can embalm my mom. That going be too rough. After giving it some thought, I said, "No, I gotta do it, because she told me, 'Make sure when I die you make me nice.'" If anything, that was the last thing I could do for her. And I figure nobody going do it better than me–because that's my mom. I just said one prayer and took care of her and everything was fine.

If it's time for you to go, you got no say. As long as you prepared, you in control of that part of your life. You're spiritually strong. You know how old folks say that life is too short? Well, I find that as I get older, the years are flying by. Life is precious, so you gotta make use of it every day. For me, I just want to spend time with my wife and kids. ❖

Moku Buchanan gets around. Born and raised on Moloka'i, he has owned a tour company and a security service, coached Moloka'i High's basketball team for four years, is a hunter, a farmer, a fisherman, a guidance counselor and even the island's mortician. The latter is an undertaking that teaches him a lot about death–and about life. "One thing I see is how well-built the human body is. Whenever I do an autopsy, I'm amazed at God's creation." Moku lives in Ho'olehua with his wife, Lori, his children, Chuckie, Aramis, Micah, Leialoha, Nainoa and Kaulana, and the family dog, Kupono.

Reny Tsark
Builder, Musician

"I always gotta remind myself, 'Eh, dummy, you making judgments again.'"

When I first got married, my wife Linda and I went to visit my sister Joanne–she live in a shack down Mokulēʻia. I was laying net, and my wife and I was walking down the beach, when I see a whole bunch of steel on the beach. I've been an iron worker for many years, so I think, "Wow, what all this steel on the beach for?"

I see one haole guy over there and he's trying to cut the steel and his torch–going pack pack pack pack. So I walk up there and I go, "Hi! What you doing with all this steel?"

And he says, "Oh, I'm building a boat."

"You building a boat? Out of steel? Wow, that's something! You need help lighting that torch?"

"Oh, you know how?"

"Oh yeah, I'm a welder." So I show him how to set up the gauges. "You got too much pressure here. And your tip dirty. You gotta clean 'em. Got a tip cleaner?"

He goes, "What's that?" So I used one of his files and I filed the thing down and I made it kinda clean.

Then he says, "How do you set the welding machine?"

I'm thinking, "Where's this guy from? You building one boat out of steel, and you don't know how to light the torch or set the welding machine?" So I helped him some more.

Now, my wife is as haole as haole can be. But, walking away, I look at her and I say, "You know the phrase 'dumb haole'? This guy gives new meaning to it." And that was judgment. I wen' judge the guy.

Well, one thing I gotta remember–it's so easy to judge people. Nowadays, I always remind myself, "Eh, dummy, you making

Reny Tsark was born and raised in Pālolo Valley "back in the dirt road days," he says. He is a builder of "whatever needs building," is a firefighter and erstwhile fire inspector, and has played slack key guitar since 1957. "My brother Sonny was my inspiration," Reny says. "In the evenings when I was small, he used to make all the kids shut up and he would play slack key in the dark." Reny lived on the beach at Mokulēʻia for two years to help build the boat in this story.

judgments again." Turns out this guy's name was Carroll Hepner and he's a nuclear engineer, and there isn't a more smart guy I ever met in my life. He's a brilliant man–just awesome.

Anyway, after that, every weekend when we go Mokulēʻia, my sister says, the Hepners want to know if you could stop by. So I start helping him out and I get real interested in this boat. So after a few weekends of going out and helping Carroll, I tell my wife, "You know what? I going quit my job, we go move Mokulēʻia."

She says, "Is that what you want to do?"

I said, "Yeah." I figure I have to test her, you know–make sure she never marry me for my money!

I was foreman for this iron worker shop and I just wen' quit. Bought one tent and live on the beach. Did that for a long time. Once I started working on that boat, I never had doubts that we could do it. I never built a boat before. I didn't even know what they called the front and the back, and here I going build one boat with this guy who don't even know how to light one torch.

One of the things Carroll Hepner wen' teach me was you get steps in everything that you do. I was learning so much from this guy that I

Reny and friends work on their huge steel boat on the beach at Mokulēʻia.

had called a "dumb haole." He never built one boat before, but he felt that if he did one piece at a time, he could do it.

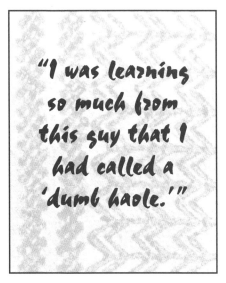

"I was learning so much from this guy that I had called a 'dumb haole.'"

He was struggling on the skill part of building it, but he knew all the figures. He had the numbers. We completed the boat and painted it. You know the water line? We painted the water line. He made a chalk line on the boat how it would sit in the water when we push it into the ocean–and he hit right on the money. Dead on the money. "Displacement," he tell me. "It's a given."

Working on that boat, we met so much interesting people. Was puka shell days back then, and people used to walk the beach picking up shells. This one guy came along one Sunday afternoon when the boat was pretty much finished. The guy–beard, pipe in his mouth–says, "What are you building?"

I look at him. "A boat."

"Yeah, that's what I thought you were building, but I didn't know steel could float."

I said, "A plane isn't made out of wood, right? If something metal can fly, then it can float."

Turned out the guy was a professor at UH. Paying all that money for an education and don't even know that metal can float! You know, I always divide "smart" and "intelligent." They two different things. Intelligent is the guys that built the spacecraft that went to the moon. Smart is when you can find an easier way to do something, when you know how to use your common sense. I don't think anybody's stupid. Some people just use their smartness and some people don't!

Well, this guy Carroll Hepner, he was smart. You no build a whole boat all at once–just do one thing at a time. That's how you do any job: one thing at a time. One little thing.

Today, this boat is massive. Eighty tons and about 72 feet long. Three stories high. You no can believe. ❖

Ralph Soken
Wall Builder

"I call this type of work 'rock therapy,' because it teaches me patience and self-discipline."

Everybody get their own style for make rock wall. Some use diamond blade to cut. That way, guarantee you get one tight fit. Look nice, like tile, but I prefer to work with the natural shape of each stone. It's all wedged together, rock on rock, sleeved in by its own weight. I use very little mortar. What cement I use is in the back, without the grout face. It's like a puzzle. It's hard to work with curves, but to me curves get flow, movement.

I call this type of work 'rock therapy,' because it teaches me patience and self-discipline. It used to be if I wished for something today, I want it tomorrow. But like with the wall, you gotta wait until the cement dries before you set the rock. Take your time.

Slowly, the lessons Naka taught me seeping in. He always said the foundation, the footing, gotta be solid. I think everything starts from there. Then, however creative you like get, at least you get the basics down. Otherwise, with the pressure of the weight pushing down, the wall going kick out. You gotta dig the footing below the grade level because if you just put the rocks right on the ground, eventually the rain going erode the soil and going undercut the wall.

Usually, I study the site before I even move the first stone. I get one idea what the finished wall going look like. I take my time to pick out the cornerstones. Hard for find the corners. You go nuts looking for the 90 degrees, but if you get the cornerstones looking good, you bring the whole wall together. The cornerstones gotta look good, plus gotta be strong.

Every stone get front, back, up and down. When you work long enough, it jumps out at you. You can see the grain. If going horizontal, you no like make 'em go vertical. You can feel if the rock belongs there. You gotta embrace it—even if it's a rock. Some days it's like nothing works, so I quit. No matter what you do, no fit. I leave it for the next day and look at it fresh again.

These days, everything's gotta be like saimin—instant. So this job keeps me in perspective. Yeah, even with stone, you gotta try work one balance—big and small. ❖

Around 1980, Ralph Soken began helping Kazuo Nakamura on weekends, digging trenches, pushing a wheelbarrow, separating and moving the heavy stones. "Naka," a third-generation rock wall builder from Japan, adhered to many of the old ways. "He didn't say much," Ralph recalls. "You had to learn by reading his eyes to know if you're doing okay or not." Naka passed away suddenly in 1986 at the age of 61, leaving Ralph to continue his unique style of construction. Since then, he has built a reputation for quality as solid as that of his *sensei*—one stone at a time.

Charlie Onaka
Rancher

"Just because it's a holiday, it doesn't mean you don't have to work."

Whether it was building our ranch or raising our kids, our family would use some of the old ways and some of the new ways to make things work. It goes back to my grandfather, who came here from Fukuoka. The story goes that when their fourth child, my uncle, was born, he was allergic to his mother's milk. He was really bad, really dehydrated, and he would have died. My grandfather had heard that cow's milk was a good substitute, so he went out and bought five or six milking cows. That's how it started, and because of all that, my grandfather might have been the first Japanese in the U.S. to own and operate his own ranch. Even when my father took over, there were no other Japanese ranchers here—only haoles and Portuguese. By then we had about a hundred head of cattle.

My father was one real cowboy. He loved to ranch. He could ride and rope with the best of them. He was one of the few who would swim his cattle out to the loading boats for ship to O'ahu. That was dangerous work; besides riding and roping from a swimming horse in the open sea, in those days was all longhorn cattle, so you could get hurt bad. But my father was a big, strong, rough man who would stand up to anybody.

Yeah, my father was one tough man. But times change, too. We weren't so rough in raising our own kids, but I always let them learn their way around the ranch by doing. They grew up working alongside me, riding, roping, clearing trees, putting up fence, branding, whateva' since they were little. They got some of the old ways: they not afraid of hard work, they show respect to elders, they know what they can do, but they smart enough to be humble; they get pride in the family name.

A third-generation cattleman, Charlie Onaka runs 1,350 acres of Big Island ranchland, high on the slopes of the South Kona Coast and near the upcountry cowtown of Hōlualoa. Part of this historic spread has been in Charlie's family since 1914, when his grandfather—an immigrant from Fukuoka, Japan—purchased a half-dozen milking cows. These days, Onaka Ranch is a fourth-generation family affair. With degrees in animal science, Charlie's nephews Bert and Kelcy help run the ranch, along with his children Kent, Kara and Kip

At Onaka Ranch, working the land is a family affair.

I guess my life can be described as lots of hard work and really loving what I do. I always wanted to be a cattleman. After I came back from college, my older brother was working the ranch with my father, so I went to work for another ranch. After my brother passed away, I didn't just inherit the ranch in the traditional way; instead, I bought it from my father, to prove that it was really important to me. I'm glad I did.

Not too long ago, my oldest son Kip came to my wife and me and said, "I want to raise papayas." At the time, he had his agriculture degree from UH and was working for the federal government as an inspector. I told him, "You sure? You get good job, steady paycheck twice a month." I didn't want him to quit, but I guess Kip is like me in many ways. When I was his age, I passed up the security of working for someone else to be one rancher. He wanted to farm.

I had one ag lease with nothing growing at the time, so I said, "Okay, you can use that to farm, but that's all the help your mom and I goin' give you. You have to do the rest by yourself."

Well, he did. First he got a part-time job, and he paid a guy to help him clear the land. He started with 50 papaya trees, then 100. Then this supermarket chain said they would buy all the papayas he can grow, so now he's going full blast. Only then his mom and I said we'd come down and help him plant. It's something he's earned.

I tell you, it's not easy to sit and watch your kids struggle. You love them; you like give them stuff; you like make it easy for them all the time. But sometimes they gotta earn 'em themselves so they know they really want 'em, that they know they can make 'em on their own–even when the going gets tough. You can't just give a kid anything he wants. If you give him a new car and he goes and busts 'em

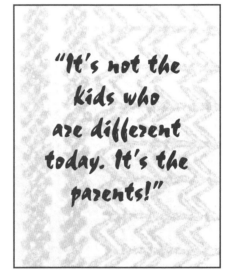

"It's not the kids who are different today. It's the parents!"

up, he figures no big deal, they'll just give me a new one. He doesn't really appreciate it 'cause he didn't earn it. It all comes down to the parents. People say, "Oh, kids today! Kids today are so different!" But it's not the kids who are different today. It's the parents!

We always tried to teach our kids the importance of hard work. Of course, it's not all work; the kids still had their sports–their baseball and football–and we were there for all their games. But, you know, just because it's a holiday, it doesn't mean you don't have to work.

My wife and I have survived some really tough times together. More than our share–drought, disease, poor prices, you name it. But like I always tell her, when you love what you do, you remember the good times. Somehow, you forget the bad and remember the good. I watch my son now, and, no matter what may come, I know he's doing what he loves to do. ❖

Mac Poepoe
Conservationist

"Smartness and knowledge are two different things. Knowledge, you develop over time."

The way we grew up, we learned by example—not too much from books. That is real important for Hawaiians. So how do you determine which is better? Who is more smart? Smartness and knowledge is two different things. I always tell my boy, "You real akamai, you get the brains, but you still no more the knowledge. Knowledge, you develop over time."

My niece, she dance with a hālau on the Big Island. One time she call me. She say she like kūpe'e shells. The people over there know she get connections on Moloka'i for go pick kūpe'e. First I say, "Okay, how much you need?" She say, "800 to 1,000." "Eh," I tell her, "first of all, you know how kūpe'e multiply?"

"No."

"You know where the kūpe'e grow?"

"No."

"Well, your kumu better go teach you guys all this kind stuff. You know Uncle no refuse you guys nothing, but this is one time I gotta refuse, because I no believe in that kind stuff. Take long time for the kūpe'e to come that big. You telling me you need 800 to 1,000? I'm sorry. I cannot do this for you." I teach the kids how to take care of the resources. You gotta learn how to take care.

We all learn different way and we get different beliefs. What I consider spiritual, someone else might not even notice. Everything gotta be balanced. We get all kind people living here in the Islands. I tell my kids, "Respect other people's identity and teach them yours, too. You know, just like the Filipino guy down the road. You no like the idea of his chicken crowing early in the morning. But, eh, maybe he no like the idea your dog always running loose scaring his chicken. So, tie up your dog—because he get his chickens in the pen. That's the balance you gotta maintain. Eh, that's my neighbor. Respect each other." ❖

Mac Poepoe grew up farming on the island of Moloka'i. A firefighter by trade, he is best known as the caretaker of Mo'omomi, a Hawaiian fishing preserve on the northwest coast of Moloka'i. Mac is an expert on ocean resources—from shoreline to deep water—when it is right to harvest, when it is not. "When I go down to the ocean, I no go only for catch fish," Mac says. "I do all my studies. I learning the ocean. The ocean more strong than me. The ocean taught me respect. Respecting that ocean—that's the only way."

Karl Bader
Retired Plantation Supervisor

"Always eat if somebody offers, no matter how strange the food. It shows you respect his ways."

One ditch way up Hālawa was 1,900 feet high. You had to walk or ride mule, for go up there. You crisscross the gulch seven times–about two miles–before you reach the lower camp.

Was hard work those days–all manpower. We carry lumber from the lumberyard–2x4, 4x4, 4x8, all the big timbers–up the mountain. When you reach the tunnels, you put the lumber inside the boat, put the lantern in the front, go in the water, and push the boat from behind. Ho, that water was cold like ice. Then, up there, we unload everything, carry 'em across the gulch on our backs.

Sometimes, danger, too. Before time was all live fuse. You light ten or 12 rows of dynamite. All you get for light was one candle. You light the fuse and the tunnel all fill up with smoke; you turn around and take off outside.

When get landslide, all the rocks come down. Every time rain, big water come down and you cannot cross the gulch. You gotta stay overnight. From the camp to the tunnel where we work was far. When big water, you cannot cross for come back, so we made wire bridge out of steel cable. You had to come back to camp on the wire.

Had one gang all Japanese contract workers. They had their own camp. My gang was all Filipinos, with one Hawaiian boy. Me, I mostly German, part Hawaiian, little bit Chinese. We all get along good. Some foremen were not so popular–they get hard time with the men–but my men was good with me. I don't know why they like me, but they tell me, "Mr. Karl, good foreman." I treat them fair, you know. I treat them fair.

One guy said, "You okay, Mr. Karl, you eat our food. The other foremen no eat our food." We had plenty new foremen–all college graduates–they come down from the mainland.

Karl Bader (with wife Anna, opposite) started working for the Big Island's Kohala Sugar in 1932 for a dollar a day. He later went to work on the hazardous Kohala Ditch project, which paid a dollar and a half. "Was hard life," he recalls, "but that was really big money." Like his father before him, Karl worked his way to the rank of foreman. In those days, plantation society was highly stratified. Management seldom socialized with the laborers— mostly immigrants from various countries. Bader was an exception who embodied the multiethnic lifestyle of Hawaii's plantation era.

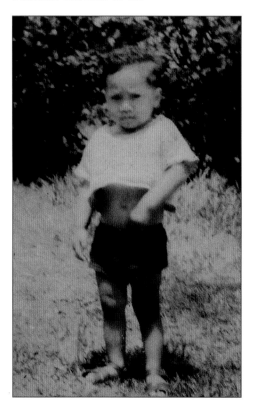

Karl's work crew dubbed his son "Big Boy,"
a nickname that stuck for life.

64

They no eat. I eat with my men. We all kau kau together. That's important—in Hawai'i or anyplace. Always eat if somebody offers, no matter how strange the food. It shows you respect him and his ways.

When we go work, all you had for lunch was two rice ball and two ume. Up there get plenty fish—big kine o'opu. We go catch, fry 'em. We used to hunt pigs, too. My gang, we go hunt all the time. They get paid for hunt. Bring back the pig; make smoke meat. They supply the camp below.

Whenever we come down, the men invite me to all their parties—wedding, baby lū'au. All what they cook I eat. The only one I no can eat is the eggs with the chick already growing inside. One time I was drinking with them, feeling good. They tell me, "Eh, Mr. Karl, try this one." I eat 'em and, ho, I wen' throw up. I tell them, "Sorry, I cannot kau kau this one." They say, "That's okay, Mr. Karl."

Working on the ditch, you really had to trust each other. Once a week or so I used to take my son up there, starting when he was only five years old. I wrap him in the raincoat, take him in the tunnel, pass through all the dikes. The men would all watch out for him. His regular name Karl, but they call him "Big Boy." That nickname stuck on him the rest of his life.

One night, the compressor broke. I gotta fix 'em; I can come down faster by myself, so I figure I had to leave the boy up there. The Filipinos and the Hawaiian boy tell me, "No worry, we take care Big Boy."

When I came down, ho, my wife scold me. "You left the boy up there?"

"No worry," I tell her. "They take care."

In the morning I take the compressor to the garage, they fix 'em, and I take 'em right back. The guys watching the boy. They made kau kau for him—everything. That's the kind of trust you had to have—to leave your son in a place like that and know he's gonna be safe. ❖

CHAPTER FOUR

Lessons in the Marketplace

W hether it's the
marketplace of commerce or the marketplace
of ideas, we have much to learn from Hawaii's
businesspeople. For these are the warriors
of our modern society, who build their successful
empires with a mix of strength and sensitivity.
They are multidimensional folks who
study the needs of a changing world and make
the right decisions to meet those needs. An
entrepreneur who finds his niche. A publisher
who works with the sick and starving. A healer
whose business spreads a message of self-help
worldwide. An architect turned cultural visionary.
Here are people who make a difference
both in their businesses and in the
community around them.

Kenny Brown
Humanitarian

"Inside every one of us is a Hawaiian."

*I*f you saw Duke Kahanamoku and asked him, "How are you today, Duke?" he might say, "Pretty good–little constipated though." Was he being crude? Not at all. He was just telling you what you asked. The secret of the Hawaiians is that we lived for so long in a time of truth.

I have a theory that the Hawaiian people are closest to the ancient ways because the last three places settled in the world were New Zealand, Rapa Nui and Hawai'i. Human beings migrated all over the world for a hundred thousand years and finally came to Hawai'i. They brought with them all the ancient wisdom and knowledge and connection with the earth and with each other. And then they were isolated here for a thousand years–a little refuge, a preserve. A thousand years the rest of the world was running around inventing guns and grabbing power and going high-tech, while Hawaiians were still interfacing with nature and each other. The Hawaiians understood that at many levels, we are all one. That's why they had so little trouble with all the various people who eventually came here.

My great-grandfather was born in the ancient way. So I'm only four generations removed from a people who lived in that time of truth. And now we are in a position to give back to the world some of that ancient universal wisdom. One way we do it is with Hawaiian music. In it you hear the surf and see the rainbows and the wind blowing the clouds across the sky.

Another way we share the ancient wisdom is through dance–one of the essential primal expressions. Music, dance, rhythm, ritual. If you can do something physical that's also spiritual, it's the greatest gift in the world. Hula is like that. Surfing can be like that too.

Hawaiians represent the compatibility of humans and we have a responsibility to teach that–but without preaching. Just watch us and we'll show you: Let's go dance! Let's go surf!

To me, this is the secret and beauty of Hawai'i. It's a marvelous, special place in the world. And now we have the job of passing it along to others. Because inside every one of us is a Hawaiian. ❖

*A*n architect by trade, Kenny Brown is a kama'āina who spent much of his childhood learning traditional Hawaiian values at Keawaiki–the family estate in South Kohala on the Big Island. From local fishermen, for instance, he learned the concept of ahupua'a–those multidimensional ecosystems stretching from the mountains to the shore and even under the sea. "We would gather at the shoreline," he recalls, "and the Hawaiians would name all the areas and districts beneath the ocean's surface." Kenny has been a State Senator and a director of countless community service groups and foundations.

Peter Gellatly
Network Media

"All you need to do is take that first step, to say 'okay.'"

PETER GELLATLY

*I*t started out as a small thing. Two little girls I met in 1990 took me to meet their families, who were living under tarps on the grounds of a mosque in Old Delhi. I took some pictures, bought milk for the babies and then headed home. When I returned to India the next year, I was drawn to the mosque again almost viscerally, like I was hooked in the belly and being reeled in. It wasn't a good scene–human waste, dead goats, sick kids running around naked–but almost everyone was still there, and we started up where we'd left off.

I began to go every morning. I'd play with the kids, take pictures, and use my terrible Hindi to learn about their lives. We'd take pedal rickshaws into the market, where I bought children's clothes, blankets, whatever seemed like it'd make life better. One morning, as I was walking to the mosque, I saw a sign on a gatepost that read, "I am the bridge from your yesterdays to tomorrow." An hour later I sat down with nine families, explained that my friendship was sincere, and asked what I could do to really help. They said, "Stop buying things. What we want is a place to live," and I said the word that changed my life: "Okay."

With that simple "okay," all things became possible. We found some land in the nearby Jumna Basti, Delhi's biggest, baddest slum, bought building supplies, and put up nine jhuggis, which are just simple thatched huts. The next year I built more and started several small businesses: rickshaws, fruit and vegetable carts, sewing machines, cigarette stands. I loaned people the money for these, with the thought that they could pay it back at just 20 rupees a day and after a year, own the business. Under one condition, that is–their children had to attend school.

Publisher, producer, community activist–Peter Gellatly is a successful Honolulu businessman who knows how to build value. The firm he founded, Network Media, is a multimedia company serving the visitor market and Waikīkī residents with magazines, books, a newspaper and television programming. But Peter's passion for building goes far beyond the boardroom. Over the past decade, he has helped improve the lives of hundreds of impoverished people in Delhi, India. Today, the Childwatch Foundation he launched in 1997 employs a staff of five and several volunteers to carry out his work in and beyond the slums.

Unfortunately, it wasn't quite that simple. Over the next few years, every time I returned to India, there was more bad news. The kids weren't going to school. Many of the businesses were failing. Some of the people either ran off with the money or sold the materials to buy food or medicine–or booze and drugs. There's a lot of addiction there. And the jhuggis were in constant disrepair because of fire and floods in monsoon season. Still, I kept on loaning and building until one year, after especially lousy news, I did something I still regret: I quit. And for the next three years I focused all my energies on my business here in Hawai'i.

Then in the spring of '97 I received word that my closest friend in the slum had died of tuberculosis and drug abuse. I was overcome with shame. I had made a commitment and hadn't lived up to it. So I returned to India, where I was overwhelmed by what I found. The people didn't begrudge my absence at all. In fact, while I was gone, three-quarters of the loans had been repaid in full, and some of the businesses were actually thriving. Better yet, children proudly showed me their report cards, proving that they, too, had kept their promises. I felt awful and elated at the same time–awful because I'd abandoned them, elated because they'd kept their word, even if I hadn't kept mine.

"Beauty and horror live side by side in the basti."

Since then, I've made a total re-commitment. We have about 50 jhuggis now, and over 50 new businesses. I built a little school. We have extensive health-care services for mothers, newborns, handicapped people and the kids, of course. I took 99 people to the clinic the last time I was there. We've started Asha Sadan, the House of Hope, on the outskirts of Delhi, where we feed, clothe, house and educate a dozen boys from the basti. Another nine boys are in a vocational school. And I'll start a girls' home soon.

Beauty and horror live side in the basti. I can remember picking maggots out of an open wound with the little tweezers in my Swiss Army knife. One six-week-old baby died in my arms, and hers wasn't the only child's body I've put in a grave. But making a difference is so easy. We've helped blind people see and lame people walk. Kids crabbing naked in the dirt a few years ago are now sitting in classrooms in their blue shorts and checkered shirts. I've had the honor of naming three newborns, one after my daughter Resham. And to be a guest, like family, at the weddings of the little girls I met originally, in the middle of the night in the middle of the slum, was amazing.

Sure, I'm proud of what our company has accomplished here in Hawai'i. But the best thing about making money is the power it gives you to do the right thing. You see this throughout our state–businesspeople trying to change things for the better, whether it's on the streets of Waikīkī or in an Indian slum. The flip side of authority is responsibility, and the busiest, most powerful people I know– the ones working 16 hours a day to make their companies better–are also the ones doing the most to help.

Success is not a goal, it's a process. And as I discovered, failure is only part of that process.

Actually, the whole thing's pretty easy. All you need to do is take that first step–to say "okay." ❖

Peter plays with a few of "his" kids: "When I'm in the basti, I feel like myself."

Dr. Ihaleakala Hew Len
The Foundation of I, Inc. (Freedom of the Cosmos)

"We are each one hundred percent responsible for our own life."

*I*first discovered the power of ho'oponopono when I took the training from Kahuna Lapa'au Morrnah Simeona in 1982. I was a staff psychologist at Hawai'i State Hospital and she had been lecturing and training at colleges, medical facilities, even the United Nations. What I learned then changed my life and I've been part of the Foundation ever since. Morrnah was our master teacher. The State Legislature honored her work by naming her a Living Treasure of Hawai'i in 1983.

Today, we conduct workshops all over the world with one basic message. And that is simply this: we are each 100 percent responsible for our own life. We create our physical universe exactly the way it is. Not only that, we each have the power to correct the erroneous thinking that can cause an imperfect reality. In other words, everything exists as thoughts in our minds. There's no "out there." It's all inside of us. We can solve all of our problems without going a single inch outside ourselves.

We call this Self I-Dentity through Ho'oponopono, the ancient Hawaiian method of problem-solving. But ours is a modern version of that process, one that relates precisely to the way we live today. The basis of this Updated Ho'oponopono is what we call "cleaning." We completely clean our minds of poisonous thoughts–those which can cause all kinds of problems–and replace them with whole, healing thoughts. And in doing so, we can restore and maintain our inner peace–spiritually, mentally and physically.

Maybe the best way to explain it is to compare it with the approach of a traditional psychologist, who treats a client with the belief that the source of the problem is with the client herself. "What's wrong with you?"

Wai'anae native Ihaleakala Hew Len graduated from the Kamehameha Schools and the University of Colorado. He went on to earn a master's degree from the University of Utah and a doctorate in education psychology from the University of Iowa. He has been a college professor, a mental health activist and a staff psychologist in the forensic unit for the criminally mentally ill at Hawai'i State Hospital. Today, as chairman of the Foundation of I, Inc. (Freedom of the Cosmos), he travels the world from his Volcano Village home–working to spread the universal message of Self I-Dentity through Ho'oponopono.

he is saying. "How can I help you correct it?" He then spends a great deal of time trying to change her thinking or her situation or anything else within her to try to solve the problem.

With Updated Ho'oponopono, however, the therapist accepts 100 percent responsibility for actualizing the problem himself. He knows that the source of the problem is the erroneous thoughts within him and not with his client. He begins the cleaning process—having his own toxic thoughts replaced with thoughts of pure Love. We call these pure thoughts the thoughts of the Original Source. Some call the Original Source Love; others call It God. Whatever you call the Original Source, It allows the therapist to begin transmuting his erroneous thoughts into love and an inner peace. The result is that his client can immediately begin to feel better. The problem might disappear. Or it might not disappear, but if his cleaning is done completely and correctly, she will accept her situation as right. I recently worked with a family whose 87-year-old mother was very sick, though the doctors could make no specific diagnosis. "Can you find what's wrong with her?" they asked me.

"We may never know why she's sick," I answered. "But one thing we do know—she is ready to leave us; her only worry is what it will to do you." Through the cleaning process, they were able to accept their mother's death as right and perfect.

The beauty of Updated Ho'oponopono is that we all have the ability to do this for ourselves. We can create our own peace without having to

Wearing his trademark baseball cap—the "P" is for the creative force, Pele—Ihaleakala takes a break with students at a seminar in Tennessee.

go to a priest or a guru or a psychiatrist. I have seen it work time and time again. We give people the specific tools for cleaning, then help them put them to work. Our students have solved an amazing variety of problems completely on their own, using the principles of Updated Ho'oponopono. After a pregnant woman does the cleaning, a medical condition with the baby she is carrying completely disappears. A mother is reunited with a long-lost daughter. A man loses his job and finds many new career possibilities.

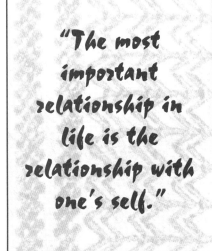

"The most important relationship in life is the relationship with one's self."

When I started at the State Hospital working with the criminally mentally ill, we had three or four major attacks between patients every day. People were shackled, put in seclusion or restricted to the ward. After months of cleaning, we saw a complete change for the better: no more shackles, no more seclusion, people allowed to leave and go do sports or work.

The acceptance of 100 percent responsibility for ourselves has special relevance for teenagers today, whose problems are really the problems of the adults in their lives. Many adults don't know their own identities, don't accept responsibility for what happens in their lives—especially the bad things. So without good adult role models, it becomes even more important for a young person to nurture the most important relationship in life—the relationship with one's self. Once that relationship is made whole, then all others automatically become whole, too.

Here's what we tell the students in our program: We are the sum total of all past thoughts, emotions, words, deeds and actions. Our present lives and choices are colored by this memory bank of the past. If we accept this, then the process of correcting and setting our thoughts aright can change our lives, our families and our society.

That's all there is to it. Your mind is its own movie projector. If you don't like the movie, you stop the projector and put in a new one. Simple as that. Believe me—it works. ❖

Allan Ikawa
Big Island Candies

"Stress is different than pressure. Stress depends on how you can handle the pressure."

We had gone through our share of hard times, but when we were hit by this crisis in 1984 we were devastated. To see all of that hard work suddenly disappear. I went to see a friend of mine from Japan. You know what he told me? He said, "Allan, samurai never give up. If you believe in what you're doing, you go down fighting to the last man. Now, your back is against the wall, you gotta fight hard." He emphasized pride as a big factor, too. You know local guys–they no like shame the family name. My wife Irma, my father, my brother had supported me all the way. Irma and I had put everything we had on the line. I didn't want to fail.

My friend from Japan said, "Now you have to see if you are prepared to handle pressure. Use your education, your experience, your spiritual training–everything that prepares you for this challenge. How you handle it is up to you."

Stress is different than pressure, my friend explained. You see, stress depends on how you can handle the pressure. Some people–like the type of basketball player that wants to take the last shot with the game on the line–they want the ball; they actually love the pressure.

Anyway, I walked out of that meeting not knowing how to feel. I don't know what I expected to find by going to see my friend in the first place–sympathy, maybe an offer to help. I might have been looking for someone to blame, someone to bail me out. I honestly didn't know. Instead, he had told me, "Everybody has to know for themselves what their breaking point is; how much pressure they can handle. You can either run away or face the music. How you deal with it is all in your heart."

The sparkling new Big Island Candies factory and showroom in Hilo stands as testament to the entrepreneurial spirit of the company's founder, Allan Ikawa. Seven years after it opened in 1977, Big Island Candies was a successful small business employing 22 people, manufacturing candy products for a major corporation. In 1984, however, that client suddenly withdrew from its agreement. Literally overnight, Big Island Candies had once again been reduced to a staff of one–Allan himself. Instead of giving up, however, he turned adversity into one of Hawaii's sweetest success stories.

> "You gotta be able to read people, who the players are, how they'll react under pressure."

As I drove back to the factory, I realized what I had to do. I rolled up my sleeves and told the workers, "Let's go. If you guys willing to stick it out, you gotta keep up with me. I'm going for it."

You know, those people that were with me from the beginning, they stuck with me through those tough times. I still have the calendar I kept during that time–marking down how many days we actually had work for them: But they hung in, called in every day, encouraged me to keep going.

I was determined to develop our own product line under our own label. I wasn't going to place our welfare in the hands of a single client again. I put in 17-hour days, from 5:30 in the morning to 10:30 at night–sometimes more. I actually put a cot in my office to catch naps when I could. Soon, our luck began to change–we developed some new products and picked up a few new accounts. Then we got the break we needed when a distributor on O'ahu called and started placing orders. When that call came, I figured I could have hung on for about two more weeks–that's it. Things had turned around for us, and we haven't looked back since.

You learn a lot about people and a lot about yourself when you go through an experience like this. I understood better than ever the importance of true relationships and trust. I read somewhere that 90 percent of your happiness is determined by who you marry. I found that to be true. If you're facing pressure at work, and then you go home and you have to face other problems, how're you gonna focus?

At work, too, you gotta get loyalty. If you don't have loyalty there's always going to be doubt. If you gotta worry about this, and you gotta worry about that, there's no way you can succeed. That's why I hire people I trust, people that going cover my back. It's so much easier to focus on what you're going to do.

In other words, you can have the best samurai swordsmen on your side, but if you don't know if they're going be there for you when you need them, what good is that? You need people you can trust 100 percent. So your friends and everybody else gotta be the good guys that going watch out for you. You cannot go floating around by yourself. You going lose.

What we try to create at Big Island Candies can be compared to a SWAT team mentality, or Navy Seals, or whatever. Everybody specializes; everybody covers each other's back.

You gotta be able to figure it out. You gotta be able to read people: who the players are, how they'll react under pressure. Do they really mean what they say? You gotta know who's out for themselves, who's going stand by you no matter what. Once you figure that out, you don't need to worry. It gets a little easier. Then work, and life in general, becomes a joy. ❖

Allan (front center) is flanked by the team that weathered the tough times at Big Island Candies.

Jonathan Lee

Chun Ha, Inc.

"Knowing when your opportunity comes and how you grab it is the whole bottom line for me."

I read in a book that everybody has three chances in their life. I believe that. My first chance came when I was age 22, so I grabbed it.

I majored in tourism and worked at a hotel for a little while, but I didn't like it. My family is three generations of fishermen, so I thought, you know, why don't I just look into fishing? It's our bloodline, so I wanted to give it a try. I went out fishing numerous times to study how the operation works. The first time I went I was sick to my stomach. Even though it's in the blood, you go out and the water is so unreal; the weather doesn't cooperate. The whole first trip I was sick–just sleep, eat, sleep, go bathroom–that's about it. The second trip was much better, because your body learns to cope.

I got my first boat back in 1994. I only had $10,000 in savings. I went to the bank to try to get a loan, but they didn't give me a chance. I had to borrow close to $200,000 from my parents, my parents' friends, my friends–wherever I can find money. That's how I started.

I was pretty lucky. I was looking at maybe three or four years to pay off the loan, but I found a good captain and the first year I was in business, I paid the loan off. The next thing you know we added two more boats and now we have a fishing supply company. It was happening so fast. Just keep going. But, with all that adversity, the main thing is taking a chance. Knowing when your opportunity comes and how you grab it is the whole bottom line for me.

I've been helping my parents since I was 14. Compared to my friends, I missed the high school days when everybody party, go to proms. I couldn't participate in most of those things because I was constantly working. I started delivering newspaper. I worked at Jack in the Box. I worked at a gas station. Because of all that experience, you know the value of the money. You know how you spend money, you know how you save money.

Some people think fishermen don't have brains–some even believe you lolo. You go out

Jonathan Lee was nine years old when his family immigrated from Korea. He quickly adapted to local life, growing up in the Papakōlea-Pauoa Valley area and attending Lincoln Elementary, Stevenson Intermediate and Roosevelt High School before graduating from Kaiser High School. Jonathan founded Chun Ha, Inc. at the age of 22. At 27, he operates three of the Islands' largest fishing boats, while his U.S. Fishing Corp. supplies bait and tackle to commercial fishermen. Jonathan has received a number of awards, including 1999 State of Hawai'i Small Business Administration Young Entrepreneur of the Year.

fish, you come back and all you do is drink and look for women. It's not like that. There's a lot of skills involved in fishing. You gotta know what you're doing. I especially respect those guys who've been fishing all their life. They're like ghosts—they can look at the water and know if the fish are living there. By looking at the colors, how the current moves. They look at the line and they know what kind of fish is coming up next—because of their experience.

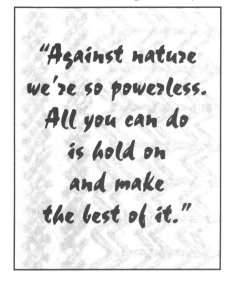

"Against nature we're so powerless. All you can do is hold on and make the best of it."

More than fight with the weather and the currents, mainly fishermen have to fight within themselves. It's all mental, you know. From when you set the line to when you pick up the line, you only sleep three hours in one day. You do that over and over again for like 15, 16 days. On top of that, there's three or four days just to go down to the fishing ground and three or four days coming back.

You're away from home. You have to leave behind your wife and your kids for a month or longer. You come back and the whole world is changing without you. It's hard. You have to find yourself within. You make like 16 or 17 trips a year. You do it for like 10, 20 years, and you get to a point where you're sick of it, but you know you have to go out. You have responsibilities. You want to provide the best you can for your family. That's the sacrifice you have to make. If you don't love what you're doing, if you're not committed, you're not going to last even one year—not just this industry, but anything you do in life.

The ocean is so vast. Sometimes we travel seven, eight, maybe ten days—just ocean after ocean after ocean. All you see is birds and clouds. It's so big and then so dark. That's why you're more with your beliefs.

In 1982, my father was out at sea when Hurricane 'Iwa hit. He was out Big Island side, trying to get away—outrun it. He was trying to make it to the Big Island, but he couldn't make it because back then we had a small wooden boat, and the speed is not so great. The boat actually went inside the eye of the storm and almost capsized. Two crewmen were swept overboard, but later that day he retrieved them safely from the ocean.

My father told me the eye of the storm is very calm. In the beginning, when the hurricane started coming, the force of the wind was unreal. And then, it was a horrific experience. You're so powerless. Even though we have so much high-tech equipment now and man runs the whole world, killing animals for food, we think we can do whatever we want, but against nature we're so powerless. All you can do is hold on.

And after an experience like that, you see the ocean differently. And then when you come home you look at life differently, too. ❖

CHAPTER FIVE

Lessons in the Arts

These are the folks
who write the songs, who see all the colors
on the wheel, who bring the good vibe.
They're the ones with the innate ability to sense,
to feel, to express themselves. You often find them
hidden beneath the quilt of society–quietly
practicing their traditions, weaving their magic.
They aren't always household names.
They could live right down your street,
around the corner–a mechanic, a meter maid,
a maintenance man. Seek their wisdom–
no shame ask. If your heart is true,
they will read it. Harness your energy and let it
direct you. You will find the art that is yours,
for through art we build character.

Frank Mamalias
Kali Maestro

"You try to correct the wrong, but you gotta do it with love, the right way, with good people."

A number of years ago, a young guy came from the mainland. He claimed he had trained in escrima with the Moro Moro in the southern Philippines. The Moro Moro are fierce people; they have never been conquered.

He arrived with many titles, trophies, articles and pictures of himself in flashy poses. He went around challenging: "There are no good escrimadors in Hawai'i." To prove his point, he tried to stage a "full contact" escrimador tournament. In the old days, this type of match could only result in either a maimed body or death. Those days, obviously, are over.

This situation was upsetting to the true teachers of escrima–"the old people," as we call them. So, I loaded up some students, teachers and elders and took them all to Waipahu. There, this guy had built an obstacle course–really playing up the Hollywood image, you know. At this event, many people from other martial arts were present, because in the past escrima has been kept in relative secrecy. Before the old people, I confronted the young man and asked him a few questions in old, southern Philippine dialect, which he would have to have known if he lived and trained there as he claimed. Well, the young man couldn't respond. It was over before it started. You see, in a warrior mindset, he was already defeated.

As soon as I did this, I told everybody, "C'mon. Bring out the food and the drinks." This is the old way–I guess you could say that the warrior strategy is to kill them with kindness. You try to correct the wrong, but you gotta do it the right way, with love. This mainland boy knew he was defeated, but we still tried to make him feel welcomed.

"The true meaning of kali," I told him, "is as a martial art. It's not a sports event." I pulled my wife and the rest of my kaoban, my family, together and stood in front of them. "This is all that kali is–to protect my family and loved ones," I explained. "I am here. If you intend to do harm to them, you must come through me." There is so much more to kali than this young man could understand, but he at least found renewed respect for the art that day. It's for protection–not for your self-esteem or ego. ❖

As a youngster growing up on Kaua'i, Frank Mamalias was immersed in the Filipino martial art of kali, otherwise referred to in Spanish as escrima. In total, he trained with 14 teachers—several of whom taught him the secrets of this ancient art. He was privileged to walk with his teachers in the forest, where he saw them do magical things. Frank was the last training partner of grand master Floro Villabrille, considered the most famous kali master of this century. And, although he shuns the title of "master" himself, Frank's skill and knowledge are legendary in martial arts circles worldwide.

Sonny D
Master Ukulele Craftsman

"We have to learn to talk with our hearts, not our minds."

I learned my lessons from my parents. My father was one wonderful man. He wen' teach me to stand like one tree. No matter how much the wind blows, I still going stand there. You can blow, blow, blow all you like, but you not going move me. I'm stronger than a rock. All the way. And all your roots, your first name, your last name, all going be just as strong, right through.

My mother wen' show me the way, too. What I learned from her I remember until today. When we was young, my friends and I stole bikes, all that kine stuff. And when we got caught, my mother wen' show me what it means to steal somebody's bike. She took my bike to Ala Moana Park and she left 'em there and of course, the next day it was gone. I never forgot that. I learned. Not because I was afraid of my mom, but because I knew how it felt. So if you only talk with your mouth with your kids, you not going get through. When you talk to one kid, you no can talk up here in the head. You gotta talk to them inside here, in their heart. And you gotta make sure the kid writes it in his heart, forever. The mind is deceiving. The eyes and the heart, that's what you gotta keep aware of all the time. The eyes see the good and the heart believes.

I was brought up in the Hawaiian way–always giving. When I was a young boy, my grandmother used to spoil me. She would give me 30 bucks and say, "Eh, go buy some clothes." One time I bought bell bottom pants–you remember in the old days. But my friends no more bell bottoms, so I buy my friend one, my other friend one, and one for me. We all get new clothes. When we got home, my mother, she don't scold me. She

In 1961 Richard Dahlin was working as a welder a block away from a Honolulu ukulele factory. At lunchtime he often visited the factory to observe the manufacturing process. "Just by watching, I would learn," he recalls. "I don't need no blueprints. I just look at 'em one time." Today, as 'Sonny D,' he is a respected master craftsman who hand-makes every one of his highly prized ukuleles. "I don't have measurements; everything is right here in my head," he explains. "I don't even have a mold for backing my ukuleles. I just use one iron, the one for iron clothes!"

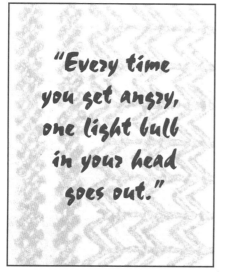

"Every time you get angry, one light bulb in your head goes out."

Hawaiian—she knows it's good to share. She just shake her head, smile and walk away. She told me, "Don't ever change—you'll go from riches to rags!" Well, she was wrong. I'm not in rags. We not rich, but we doing okay. I don't want to become rich. I just want to be just right. And the only way to do that is you gotta keep giving, giving, giving and don't stop.

Even when you chance getting ripped off, you have to be willing to give. Like the guy who came over here from Japan and bought $3,000 worth of ukuleles. He says, I'll take the ukes and I goin' send you one check. So he take the ukes and no send nothing back. Rip off. But, you know, I no can get mad at the guy. That's the kind of thing you gotta think about before you let him go in the first place. I not goin' die for $3,000 worth of ukuleles. I not gonna hit the guy for the $3,000. Not worth it.

Or when we used up all our money for fix our broken-down garage roof. Afterwards the roofing guys took off and went back to the mainland. Six months later I look up and big hole! Turns out had one whole nest of termites and the guys never tell us. Just wen' cover 'em up. But still, I cannot hate the guys.

Getting ripped off is like drinking a glass of water. You drink it down, you digest, it's gone. No sense worrying any more about it. You cannot feed yourself bad stuff. You do that and your body goin' get all jam up. Every time you get angry, one light bulb in your head goes out. Then you get stress, you get one stroke, or diabetes, or you need one quadruple bypass. So you gotta learn how to swallow 'em, so the thing goes down and goes away.

I believe if you don't keep giving, you lose. One time had this Filipino kid downstairs, playing ukulele. One junk ukulele, cheap kine. But he can really play. Every morning he play and all the kids put their books and down and watch him play—and they singing too. So I tell my son, "Look around the shop. Get one ukulele around here someplace, one extra one?"

"Yeah, in the back, Dad."

The next day I gave the boy one brand new concert ukulele. But when he took the uke home, his mother and father came back over here, because they thought the boy wen' steal the ukulele. I told them, "No, I gave him the uke."

We have to learn to talk with our hearts, not our minds. I figure we give away hundreds of ukuleles. I cannot give plenty one time, but I can give one, one, one—one for every school on the island.

We human beings were made to love each other, to help each other. We should never get bored, because we're so busy loving our neighbors and helping them. We should be happy just to hug them and do something for them. How many times can you get to do that? ❖

Sonny D strums one of his signature ukuleles.

Atsuo Nishioka
Kendo Master

"What's right is right, even if sometimes you have to suffer for it."

*I*n 1969, our kendo club swept the state tournament. We brought home 21 out of 25 possible trophies and medals. After we came home, I thought to myself, "That is that. That is done. Now we gotta take one different direction." I wrote on the board for the teachers: "Kendo, fighting spirit." You train not only to win tournaments, but for fighting spirit, character building and the pursuit of beautiful kendo.

I got lots of backlash. Some of my assistant instructors quit. They said, "Eh, Nishioka, something wrong with the way you teach kendo; the club don't win tournaments anymore." The parents fought me. Many pulled their kids out of the club. I even had trouble with the other kendo hall.

First I thought, "What did I do wrong?" I had to ask, "What are we in kendo for?" I felt we weren't doing anything wrong, so I never quit. I get more set in my direction.

When you train only to win, you only practice what you like—what you're good at. You don't emphasize what you're weak in. That way, you don't need a teacher. You know it all. You close yourself off to everything else.

Classical kendo focuses on repetition—repeating the basics. It's real rigorous training. At the time, you don't think you're accomplishing anything, but, eventually, it helps. It helps you with hand speed, foot speed—it helps you with every aspect of the art.

If you relate this to life, I guess the point is to repeat the basics of life. Respect, patience, humility—you have to practice them all of the time—over and over. It's a long, drawn-out process. People don't seem to have that patience anymore. We teach our students that the spirit not only applies to kendo, it has to run throughout your daily life. You gotta have spirit in the family, in your work, at school and so forth.

Throughout my life, I got into a lot of trouble because I'm not the kind guy that can look the other way. I believe what's right is right, even if you might end up suffering for your actions. If you're always agreeable, nobody bother you. Kendo has helped to keep me honest and very direct. I can walk around with my head up and my chest out. ❖

Atsuo Nishioka started his kendo training when he was 12 years old. "Before the war, every community had a kendo hall," Atsuo recalls. When World War II broke out, however, everything Japanese was shut down. Kendo was banned. "Whatever kendo gear we had, we either buried 'em, threw 'em away or burned 'em." After the war, Atsuo put in 23 years in the construction industry before becoming a building inspector for Hawai'i County. "I needed exercise," he says, "so that's when I went back into kendo. What little equipment we found was old, pre-war equipment. We patched up what was left and got started."

Mae Akeo Brown
Hula Dancer

"The real mana is to love what you're doing."

T he show first started in 1937 at Sans Souci Beach. The Kaimana Beach Hotel wasn't even there yet. What a beautiful spot, just like a postcard with the grass shack and the steamship *Lurline* or *Matsonia* parked offshore. It was a very small show then, just once a week, on Tuesday, with only five or six girls dancing in a little arena in front of these wooden bleachers. It got bigger and we did it more often later on, when our founder, Fritz Herman, started going around to the hotels and leaving little signs on the front desks, telling people about the show. Then we moved over by the Waikīkī Shell after the war. That canoe has been with us for the better part of the years. And the tikis, too. They followed us around.

I was only 12 years old when I started with the Kodak Hula Show. My Auntie Louise Silva collected her nieces to dance. I was going to St. Augustine School in Waikīkī and the sisters weren't really happy about my leaving school in the morning and then coming back. But later when I was at McKinley, the principal, Dr. Carey, was a wonderful man who loved hula and told me, we're privileged to have you in our school.

The show was a family thing then and it still is a family thing. Auntie Lou trained me and my cousins and brought in some other teachers, like Uncle Joe Ilalo'oli, who was a pioneer of the ancient hula and chants. Besides playing at the show, we traveled to the military installations and hospitals as a community service. I learned to play the guitar and, later on, the bass and the ukulele.

For six decades Mae Akeo Brown has been a dancer and singer at the popular Kodak Hula Show. Performing on the beach at Waikīkī and in nearby Kapi'olani Park, the sprightly entertainer has danced and played for millions of visitors-- group tours and the carriage trade alike. A Honolulu native, 73-year-old Auntie Mae comes from a long line of well-known entertainers, including her mother, Jenny Akeo, who sang for years as Jenny Kealoha with the Royal Hawaiian Band and helped launch the Kodak Hula Show. These days the show is funded and operated by the Hogan Family Foundation.

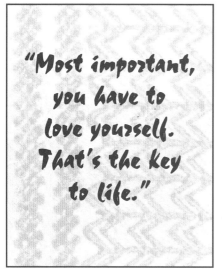

"Most important, you have to love yourself. That's the key to life."

We also used to perform for the actors and actresses who came over and stayed at the Royal Hawaiian Hotel. My autograph book was loaded with all those people! Jean Harlow and her mother would invite us up to their room to entertain after our show. I remember I taught Jean Harlow "Little Brown Gal" and a hula, "Holoholo Ka'a," which she had a hard time learning. What a nice lady she was—pretty, pretty, pretty!

This business isn't always easy. If a girl wants to dance in the show, I'm glad to sit down with her and tell her what's expected. I warn them, your kumu hula may not be easy to work with. "That's okay," they say, but of course, next thing you know, they come to me and they're crying. Then I tell them crying is very, very good, because then I know you're learning. Otherwise, maybe you're only in it for a little fun, or to make a little money. And another thing, I say, don't go thinking you're going to have the best part in the show. No one girl is better than another. Before you can be the star, you've gotta show me that you love what you're doing. Then you can dance for me anytime. Anybody can—whether they're Hawaiian or whatever their nationality is.

When I was learning, I didn't have the privilege of deciding that this is what I want to do for the rest of my life. Auntie Lou said this is what you're going to do, and so I learned to narrate in two weeks. But learning all the hulas was really tough. We had to memorize so much so quickly. I worked hard at it, and I cried because my legs, my knees, were so sore. You know how it is—up, down, here, there, everywhere! Uncle Joe, our kumu, taught me for about a year-and-a-half, and when he was done with me, I had the most graceful hands! What's important is to have a good understanding with your kumu—what he would like to get out of you and what you can do.

If you have that, it's the greatest thing, because he can teach you about hula and he can teach you about life, too. I remember Uncle Joe saying, "Life is not something you kick around like a ball. No, you have to decide what you want to be, what you want to do with your own life."

What you learn in hula should go right to your heart. You keep it there and you love it there. All the kumu hulas I know, everything comes from the heart. I know how hard they work, what they put into it, and when I watch the Merrie Monarch Festival, I think too bad they all cannot win.

Later on, I never took money for training the new kids. I get paid enough just by doing what I'm doing. And this way, I know they'll do what I ask them to do. You know, when people have to pay, they can get kinda fussy. They'll say, that's not what I want to learn!

The Kodak Hula Show has been wonderful for me. I'm 73 years old, and it's been my life. But performing like this really has to be within your heart. You gotta love it 'cause if you don't, it would be just another show. I love every show I perform in. Because the real mana is to love what you're doing. That's the best thing for any entertainer—or anybody!

Most important, of course, you have to love yourself. That's the key to life. And smile a lot. You have to smile. I smile plenty. ❖

Hogan Family Foundation

In its infancy the Kodak Hula show was held on Sans Souci Beach, a seashell's throw from the Natatorium (right rear).

Martha Hohu
Kupuna

"If you didn't understand, you said nothing."

I'm grateful to be able to survive and minister as best I can to the children. When the kids want to know something and they can't find it, they call. That's what I'm here for. I know some kūpuna don't want to answer, then they blame the young people for making mistakes. I feel we should share with them what we know while we're living; we're to blame if we refuse to answer them.

My mama and papa both spoke Hawaiian–that was all they spoke. In the Hawaiian way, the process of learning was you sit and you listen. When it came to language, they would speak in front of us all the time. If you didn't understand, you said nothing. After you hear it repeated, then pretty soon you get it. If you still couldn't figure it out, you waited for the right opportunity to ask your questions. It was not proper to interrupt with unnecessary questions. That process taught you patience and discipline–it taught you to be thoughtful and exact in what you asked for and what you said. It taught you to respect truth–to speak the truth and then to receive the truth back.

People are so impatient these days. If my moʻopuna, keikis–anybody– have a question, they usually want to know the answer right away. And then they are willing to settle for any answer. My mama and papa taught me to tell the truth. If people ask me something I don't know, I don't fake it! I tell them I don't know. There are many times when I have to say, "I cannot answer now. Give me time and I will find it for you or refer you to someone who can help you."

By being truthful, it teaches them to trust you and to feel comfortable coming to ask again. That trust teaches them discipline and patience to wait for a true answer–it teaches them to be careful how they say things and what they say. That is the Hawaiian way. The many values Mama and Papa taught us, I have taught to my children, and they have taught their children. That's the legacy. ❖

Martha Hohu is one of Hawaii's most respected and beloved *kūpuna*. She is frequently consulted on many things Hawaiian—including matters of language, nature and music. She has been a music teacher all of her life, sharing her knowledge as a choir arranger, piano teacher and music instructor at the Kamehameha Schools—from which she graduated in 1926. Her legacy has been carried on by her daughter, Leila Hohu Kiaha, who has also assumed her mother's directorship of the Kalaupapa Choir Group and as organist and choir director at Kaumakapili Church.

*Mary Lou Kekuewa and
Paulette Kahalepuna*
Feather Lei Artisans

"Every morning, Paulette and I hold hands, and we pule before we open that door."

This is not easy to talk about, but if it helps someone else, I'm willing to share. At one time, alcohol was like my food. It kept me going from day to day. You just feel so good at the time, you know. No troubles; everything is beautiful, but you don't realize what you're doing–how you're hurting the ones you love.

Twenty years ago, Paulette and I went to the Aloha Week ball, you know, mother and daughter Aloha Week queens. Well, I got to feeling high that night, and I got up the next morning not remembering too much. I could sense there was a great uneasiness about the house, so I asked my husband, "Was I all right last night, Daddy?" And he said, "Yeah, I guess. No more than the usual."

I broke out into a cold sweat, thinking, "What did I do?" I went upstairs to see Paulette. I apologized to her. I said, "You know, baby, I will never take another drink as long as I live because I love you." She said, "No, Mom, you don't have to do anything that drastic."

But I could feel this unhappiness that I was causing in the house where we all lived together–the house that my mother gave me, that I was raised in. When everybody else in our family moved away, I never left my momma. Then, when she died, my daughter came and stayed with me. Now, we're both widowed so we depend on each other.

I stopped that day, 20 years ago–cold turkey. It was hard. There were times when Paulette would say, "No, Momma, just take a few to make yourself feel better." But I'd say, "I love you baby, and you know where Momma is at now–I cannot take only a few. 'Just a few drinks' would turn into a few bottles."

Mary Lou Kekuewa first ran for Aloha Week Queen in 1955. Although she didn't win the title that year, she began volunteering at the Aloha Week office. There, she learned the art of feather lei making. "That's how it started," says Mary Lou, "and I've never stopped. Now, we have four generations doing this work." In 1970, Her daughter Paulette was named Aloha Week Queen. And, in 1975, Mary Lou finally realized her dream and was crowned queen herself. Today, mother and daughter own and operate their own Hawaiian feather shop in Kapahulu, Na Lima Mili Hulu No'eau.

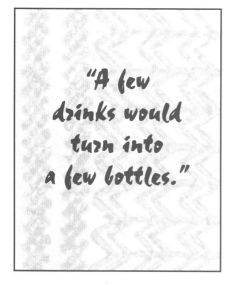

"A few drinks would turn into a few bottles."

I'm so glad that I have Paulette to fall back on because there were many times when I needed to talk to somebody and my husband, Paul, was never around. He was a tugboat captain, so when I said goodbye to him, I never knew when I was going see him again. He was a good husband, don't get me wrong, but he was gone so much.

Eight years ago, we started this business together. Every morning for the past eight years, Paulette and I sit together, we hold hands, and we pule before we open that door. Twice in those eight years, she wouldn't let my hand go. She'd say, "What's wrong, Mother? Why are you upset? Did I say something to hurt you?" And I'd say, "No, it's okay." But she wouldn't let go of my hand, "No, it's not okay, Momma. Before we open that door, we have to be all right." So then we talked about what we felt. Then, after we understood each other, she said, "Okay, Mom," and we reach across, we kiss each other. "Okay, pau." Then we open the door and we're in business.

People can't believe we're in the store 12 to 14 hours a day. I say, "That's right. And when we go home we stay in the same house." We do. If it wasn't for my love for my daughter, my fear of losing her, I would still have an alcohol problem today. I mean, really, I wouldn't even be able to hold a needle and thread–but I can because of her. ❖

CHAPTER SIX

Lessons in Teamwork

Everybody knows what athletics teaches us. The message is hammered home—with authority!—by coaches every day: Listen up, team! There's no room for whining here, no time for self pity. Learn from the past but don't dwell on it, because the next play is coming right at you. Practice, practice, practice—improve those skills. Learn to roll with the punches, to adjust to situations, to make decisions under pressure. Play hard, but respect the other guys. Believe that you can make a difference—as an individual and as a part of the whole. That's the real key to teamwork. Okay, break's over! Get out there and show me some hustle!

Pal Eldredge
Coach and Teacher

"I'm not going to go back and yell at my class because we lost a baseball game."

Baseball teaches so much more than just how to play a game. There's character, discipline, preparation, tradition, building self-esteem and improving yourself not just as a player but as a person—everything from how you act on the team bus to how good a bench player you are. Maybe you don't play every day, but you still gotta be the best bench guy there is—mentally and physically prepared so that when you get your chance, you'll produce as much as you possibly can. If you're satisfied with just sitting on the bench, then you shouldn't even be there.

But one of the best lessons is how to keep the important things in your life—family, school, sports—separate from each other. Maybe a kid gets in a fight with his girlfriend one night. He's so upset he doesn't study. The next day, he comes to class, flunks a test and doesn't turn in a paper. He gets busted for that, so now he's 0-and-2, right? His girlfriend is mad at him and now his parents are mad at him for flunking. Now he goes out to the field, lets out all his anger, and now his coach is mad at him. So now he's like 0-for-4 right there.

And so I tell him, "Try to put lines in between these things. So you're having a fight with your girlfriend? Eh, I'm sorry about that. But you learn to live with it and then you go on to the next phase of your life, okay? One thing at a time. One day at a time."

There are days when our Punahou team loses a game in the bottom of the seventh inning on a last-second home run. Thirty minutes later I have to ride into Rainbow Stadium on my motorcycle, shower, get on TV in front of 200,000 people watching Rainbow baseball and then be like there's nothing wrong. I can't say, "Well, too bad today, Jim, we just got the crap kicked out of us by St. Louis." No, I've gotta separate it. You lose or you win—eh, terrific. Now, I go on to the next part of my life. I'm not going to go back to school and yell at my class because we lost the baseball game. Everything is separate. ❖

Pal Eldredge is something of a local Renaissance man. The Punahou School and Brigham Young University graduate has been a Punahou teacher and head baseball coach for more than 30 years, handles play-by-play and color commentary for University of Hawai'i sports broadcasts, is a Harley-Davidson buff and a well-known Island musician, and still has time to pursue his passion for golf. What's more, his extensive collection of Island baseball memorabilia is second to none.

Dean Kaneshiro
Coach and Counselor

"They're not going to get better at academics or anything else unless they feel good about themselves."

I went from teaching and coaching at McKinley High School to working with at-risk kids in the Special Motivation Program at Dole Intermediate. It was a tough adjustment. These kids real kolohe, so my goal was to get them disciplined. In the beginning, I thought you have to make it real tough. After a while, though, I realized something was missing. In high school–teaching, coaching–at the end of the year you felt appreciated. Now, because I set myself up to be the bad guy, nobody ever said to me, "Eh, thanks for being tough on me."

I had to change my approach. I had made them listen, but that's not enough. They weren't going to get better at academics or anything else unless they felt good about themselves. So my goal became to build up their self-esteem.

First, I had them do campus beautification projects–take pride in their school. But the connotation was, "You guys in trouble; you probably was the ones who messed it up anyway."

I had to work with the kids in a setting where they could just be themselves, so I took them to preschools and senior citizen centers. Working with the seniors and little kids, they not going show off; they don't have to act macho; they have nothing to prove.

I told them, "When we go there, you're going to be the teachers." For Halloween, we made masks, small goodie bags. Working with the little kids, a different side of them comes out. They feel appreciated. And it was real touching to see the young kids hugging these students before they leave. I don't know how often these guys and girls get hugged.

My hope was that this positive feeling would transfer back to a school setting. For some it worked. For some it didn't. Maybe it registered years later. I see some of them around now and they say, "Remember when we made the haunted house and invited all the little kids?" When they reflect like that, I think it must have done something for them. It's that sparkle in their eye. I can see it in them: "That was good. I feel good." ❖

Dean Kaneshiro learned about "tough love" as a standout football player at McKinley High School. "Coach was always on my case, pushing me to get better. Sometimes, I got upset. But it wasn't personal. He'd tell me: 'I'm doing this because I like you. If I didn't, I'd just let you go and act like a fool in front of everybody. I'm trying to help you.' Later on, I came to appreciate what he did for me." Everything Dean has done in his adult life has been aimed at helping people: as a high school football coach, teaching at-risk kids in middle schools, and helping adults who want to learn to lift weights and improve their health.

John Sharp
Football Coach

"Wherever we go, they say, 'Oh, here comes Pālama Settlement in that green truck.'"

One of the things that sold our program was our academics. All of the kids that play at Pālama have to earn the opportunity to play by doing their academics. They have to go to the learning center and get that right before they come out to the field and practice. It's amazing how kids will put out when they see all this stuff going for them—like the grades, the discipline, being nice at home, treating your parents properly. All these things make that individual into a super human being, a super athlete.

By the time we got to games on a Saturday and Sunday, nobody there knew what those kids had gone through to get to that point. They got out there and played, man. They couldn't believe it, because we played like high school. We didn't play like Pop Warner. We played like high school.

We had discipline. We used to psyche the other teams out. We had that big green truck, "cattle truck," they call it. That psyche everybody out. Wherever we go, they say, "Oh, here comes Pālama Settlement in that green truck."

We'd pull in and all our guys would fall out. Nobody say a word. Never. Nobody mouthed. Once they got out, everybody gave me a big hug. You see, the relationship between a coach and his players has got to be a loving kind of relationship, you know. And every one of my players hugged me before every game, man. It was just a matter of caring, and they'd go out there and do their best for me. You see.

After we got off the truck, we might sit in the center of the field, or somewhere near the field—nobody still not saying anything, just sitting in a circle. I have them just close their

John Sharp was a football standout at Michigan State University. After a brief stint with the NFL Detroit Lions, John was drafted into the Army in 1964 and stationed at Schofield Barracks. He moved back to Detroit after completing his two years of military service, but devastating race riots convinced him that Hawai'i was where he belonged. Returning in 1966, he worked at the Kalihi YMCA before joining Pālama Settlement in 1968. John is the winningest coach in Hawai'i Pop Warner football. From 1969 to 1979, Pālama's record was a dominating 96-3-1. John is now recreational supervisor at the Hawai'i Job Corps.

> "When I smelled the paint on his shirt, I had to make a decision."

eyes and do some deep breathing. The other team and coaches are being psyched out. I'm messing with their heads, man. So we'd jump out there 20 to nothing the first quarter.

I taught all my players—everybody—do their job. All 40 players, everybody will learn how to play. I played everybody. I get to the state championship games out at the stadium, and I might start my third team. I didn't care. Although the talent wasn't as great, they could go out there and do the job. My third team go out there and do as well as my first.

One time, we were going to play Waimānalo for the championship. Our starting quarterback was also the quarterback at Farrington High School. But he was into sniffing paint. I smelled the paint when he first came down to play for me. I caught him the first day we had tryouts. I said, "Hey man, you can't play for me if you're going to sniff that paint." He said, "Okay, coach, I'm not going to sniff the paint." So, as the season went on, I never smelled it on him until this one big game that we were getting ready to play.

He's my number one man. We sure don't want to lose him, because we got a chance to go for the big one. The winner got a trip to Disneyland, and the kids wanted it real bad. But I had already told him three months ago that he can't get high on paint. So when I smelled it on his shirt when he came in, I had to make a decision.

I called him over and I said, "You can't play on Saturday." He said, "Why, coach?" I said, "I smell it." He started crying, "Coach, please!" I said, "No, you can't play, because I think it's more important that you understand that what that paint is doing to you is taking this game away from you, buddy. You know your choice was either to play this game or sniff this paint. You chose to sniff the paint. I don't even want you at the game."

We were a little shaky about it because we didn't know how our second team quarterback would do, especially in such a big game. Man. We went out there by the airport—at the Keʻehi Lagoon field—and we won 55 to 7 with our second team quarterback. Then we went on and played at the stadium and won our trip to Disneyland.

Of course that was quite an experience, too, for this young man. He thought that we couldn't do without him, but we went out there and the kids played harder than ever before, man. I mean, they knew they had to play hard, plus they wanted to go to Disneyland, too. They were so disappointed with the quarterback, man. I mean, just totally disappointed.

At the time, you never know for sure if they learned their lessons well enough. I've had both successes and failures. But Pālama Settlement saved a lot of these kids who were headed for trouble, man. Now, when I run into guys, they're already adults. I see them out here now and a lot of these brothers are doing real good. That's my reward. ❖

In the 1970s John was a popular football coach at Pālama Settlement.

Dennis Agena
Basketball Coach

"All the kids I coached through the years are my kids."

We always treat the players equally–from stars to less-talented players. Kids are not dumb; they can see and feel favoritism. My coaching philosophy has always been to win the respect of the player by always being honest and fair. If they respect you and you respect them, you'll see how hard they will work for you, and how truly humble you become.

Age makes no difference in my clinics–it's commitment and attitude. Every player develops at their own pace. We first start them all together, then we break into groups and work on different skills. If a seven-year-old has exceptional skills I'll move him to the next level. If a 13-year-old lacks particular skills I'll tutor him at the level he can work at until he is ready to move to the next level. I tell a player where they are at and what he needs to work on. I tell him not to get discouraged just because a younger kid moved up. That kind of understanding teaches you honesty–honesty to yourself and honesty to others.

My wife and I don't have our own children, so all the kids I coached through the years are my kids. It's a really good feeling when I look back and remember certain kids that got into a lot of trouble, and I helped to pull them through and guide them through sports. I see them today and they have become decent citizens–working hard, raising a family. I was part of their life. That's why I work with kids–because it's important to make an impact during the formative years, and basketball can shape them.

I guess I'm driven to be there for the kids 'cause when I was eight years old my mom died, and my dad was never there. When I was playing sports, I had no guardian or parent, nobody to support me or guide me, not until I was about ninth grade. Two of my greatest mentors at Kalākaua–Herb Yasuhara and Saburo Kondo–they gave me the attention I needed. Kids just need attention. They always told me to keep working at it and never give up. I promise to continue their legacy. So I'm 51 years old–and still going. ❖

In basketball circles, Dennis Agena's name is synonymous with Kalākaua Gym, where he coached from 1966 to 1998. Now an assistant coach at Kamehameha Schools, Dennis is well-known for his highly successful youth basketball clinics at Kalākaua, Kalani High School and Seabury Hall on Maui. Of the thousands of kids who have completed his program, approximately 90 percent have gone on to play high school ball. Among the notables: Nani Cockett, Melanie Azama, Blane Gaison, Ia Sapaia, B.J. Itoman and Kirk Uejio.

Blane Gaison
Pro Football Veteran

"I'm not interested in what I've done. I'm interested in where I'm going."

The choices that I made in the past put me where I am today, and the choices and the attitudes that I make today will determine where I go tomorrow. I've always wanted to be the very best that I could be. In order for me to do that I have to make the right choices. Every morning you get up, you have choices.

For example, after five years in the NFL, I had to make a decision whether to go on playing or not. I had the opportunity to continue. I wasn't told I couldn't play anymore. It's a lot of work and there's a lot of risk involved in it, but the money is very good. If it came down to a matter of economics, I would've played another five years. I felt fortunate to have been in the league for five years. I had something that a lot of people dream of having. But I had suffered some injuries and I just had my son and, all of a sudden, a light went on. I knew it was time to move on to another stage of my life.

I look at some of the friends that I played ball with—guys that continued on for another four or five years after I retired—and half of them can't even walk straight today. They have to walk with canes and so forth. When I look at that, I know I made the right choice. I have no regrets.

Once you make a decision you gotta move forward with it. Even if you make a wrong decision, you learn from it, and you continue on—period. You always have to make the best of a situation and look at it with a positive frame of mind.

One day, my daughter came home from school all excited. She was talking to some of the teachers and they had said some very positive things about me. She came home,

There is little that Blane Gaison has failed to achieve in his remarkable athletic career. When he graduated from Kamehameha in 1976, he had won high school All-America honors in football, baseball and basketball. During his sterling collegiate football career with the University of Hawai'i Rainbows, he was named All-American in 1980 and 1981 and was voted co-MVP in the 1981 Hula Bowl all-star game. Blane then played five seasons for the National Football League Atlanta Falcons from 1981 to 1985. He is presently co-athletic director at the Kamehameha Schools.

In the National Football League, Blane spent five years with the Atlanta Falcons.

very proud, and she asked me, "Well, what do you think about that, Dad?"

I said, "It's nice to know they had good things to say. It makes me feel really good, but that doesn't concern me a whole lot. I'm not interested in where I was or what I've done. I'm interested in where I'm going. That's what you need to focus on." I see too many people who get caught up in how things used to be or what they used to do.

When I was growing up, my mom and dad always told us, "Whatever you do, you always want to do your very best. Whether it's studying, playing sports, being a friend, you always want to give your very best."

Because of this upbringing, I've never been afraid of hard work. I've never backed away from a challenge. I've always wanted to be the very best at whatever I did. And the only way you gonna get there is to continuously raise your standards.

When you look at athletes like Michael Jordan, Magic Johnson, Brett Favre and people like that, what really stands out to me is that they are always taking it to another level. They're never satisfied with their past accomplishments. Once it's done, it's history. It's time to move on to new challenges. To me, it's most important to maintain a positive attitude and your inner drive to continuously find ways to get better. ❖

CHAPTER SEVEN

The Lessons of Kalaupapa

Kalaupapa creates
mixed emotions. It's a place so fragile,
you don't want to tell a soul about it. And yet,
you want everyone to know. It's the place where
society tried to isolate pain, sadness, ugliness.
And yet, today there is no ugliness, only beauty.
Here, there are no tears of sadness, only tears
of joy. The people of Kalaupapa have learned
to accept life–unequivocally.
Sit quietly with them and feel their passion
for life, the depth of their beauty. Anyone
privileged enough to visit leaves with the joy of
simply being alive, and with gratitude for
whatever hand life has dealt them. Kalaupapa is
a Hawaiian place so special, it deserves
its own separate chapter.

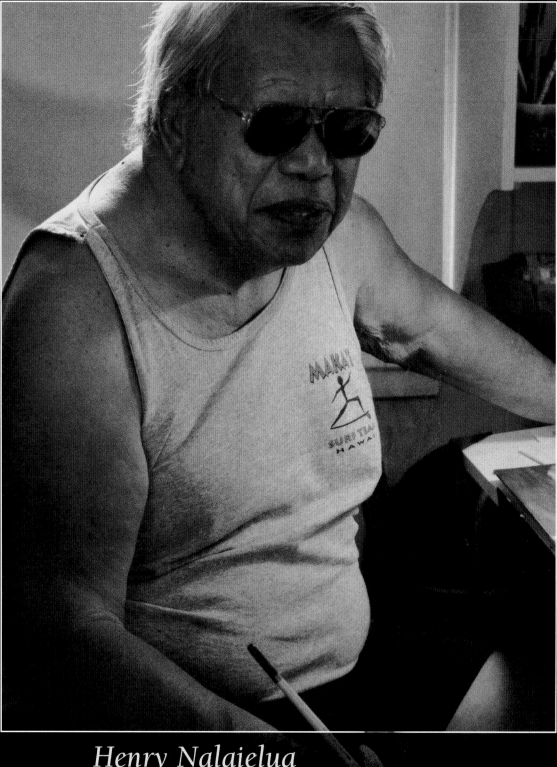

Henry Nalaielua
Kalaupapa Pioneer

"I like my life the way it is. I ain't goin' change it now!"

I came to Kalaupapa right before the the war, on September 22, 1941. I was only 15 then. The hospital in Honolulu was full to overflowing. We had to double up in the rooms there and so we started getting our letters from the Board of Health saying, you going on the next shipment, whether you like it or not.

Life was very different here in those days. I remember my first night sitting at the supper table and watching this guy who was smoking. I seen him inhale but I no see smoke coming out his nose; I seen it coming out his throat! When we first came here, all the old-timers told us if you can pass seven years, then you lived a long time. If you no take care yourself, then after seven years–you dead. That was no joke. The people here had already figured out the life span by their own calculation. They had seen so many people come up, shipment after shipment after shipment, that they knew exactly. So I figured, what the hell, I'll be lucky if I live seven years. Well, I been here 58 years. Of the 39 people in the group I came up with, there's only four of us left.

Those old-timers had the disease for a long time, and most of them were unrecognizable. They weren't active–no go fishing, no go mountains, no go no place because they cannot. But us young guys, we were clean, we were anxious, we were jumping all over the place. When we came here, there were a few young ones like us who took us around. I got here on Tuesday, on Wednesday I was fishing. Pretty soon we became 'ohana, like being adopted.

The old-timers used to tell me stories of how things were when they first came, when things weren't so pleasant as they are now.

*F*ramed by towering cliffs and the wave-tossed Pacific, the hamlet of Kalaupapa was once a place of stark tragedy and human suffering, as leprosy patients from throughout the island chain were cast into the waters off the windswept Makanalua Peninsula. Today, however, Kalaupapa's few remaining residents live there not in exile but out of a deep attachment to the land. When they are gone, their lush, scenic home will be rezoned for public use. Henry Nalaielua has made his home at Kalaupapa for nearly six decades—fishing, guiding tours and playing an active role in community affairs.

"Today, we have a lot we can teach here at Kalaupapa."

You see, when Kamehameha V first decreed that this place would be set aside for people with this disease, there were Hawaiians living here. But they were angry with the king for making them move out, and they left everything in a shambles when they went. So when the old-timers arrived, they could only build makeshift shelters with the lumber lying around. Or they had to live in the bushes or up in the trees or in caves. It was a struggle just to get medicine or proper clothing. You were just dropped off on the beach, given nothing, told nothing. And if you had a bad hand or bad leg, what could you do? There were no doctors, no nurses, no sterile dressing. They would tear their own clothes into strips to bandage themselves. You couldn't get better, only worse. The life expectancy then was between six and 11 months.

When the real doctors came here, they were with the United States Public Health Service and they built our first hospital, one of the most modern hospitals in the Territory of Hawai'i. So then they had this beautiful facility but nobody to work there. The people who came to work were afraid. There was one brilliant technician who worked in the lab. When he went to Honolulu, he got himself a girlfriend. But when she found out where he worked, she was even more afraid than him, and she told him to quit. He never came back. That's the kind of strain they would go through.

Back then, when we thought about the future: zero, nothing. You no can see as far as from here to the window. But after the war when the drugs came, we could finally look forward to getting better. We could finally say, yes, there is hope. That's when life changed. I would say about 90 percent of us got better. Then in 1969, they changed the law, said that no new patients can come here. Anyone found with this disease today can be treated as an outpatient.

Myself, I haven't been on the medication since 1960. I like my life the way it is. I ain't going to change it now!

Today, we have a lot we can teach here at Kalaupapa. Not too long ago we had a class of slow-learning children come visit. They came here to learn. At first I thought, how do you handle kids? We never had any here. Can we control them? Can we keep them out of people's places? But this was a good bunch of kids who were willing to learn, willing to sit down and listen. We taught them things about nature here, how things were formed. What we can do to get rid of pollution. We went to the beach and picked up debris and talked about where it came from. They were excited–they never saw water like this before, so clean.

Whatever we had to offer, they didn't take it for granted. They took it as something that had meaning for them. Both the kids and their leaders were enriched with who we were, what we were and what we had to teach. This turned out to be a wonderful place for them, especially now that the place is more open. ❖

Hawai'i State Archives

Early Kalaupapa residents received spiritual guidance and medical care from Belgian priest Damien de Veuster and later, from the U.S. Public Health Service.

Clarence "Boogie" Kahilihiwa
Kalaupapa Resident

"The kūpuna only tell me,
'Hoo, boy, you nīele, you nosy!'"

Kalaupapa in the old days, everybody was close. Everybody come together as one community.

One thing when I wen' come to Kalaupapa, though, the old kūpuna no like listen to the young people talk. You gotta let the young people be heard, too. Today, because I was one of the young ones in Kalaupapa in those days, I tell my wife, "I think I can be the filter for the young people." Speak on their behalf, you know?

Young people can get intimidated by the kūpuna, because they always told, "Neva' mind." In the traditional Hawaiian way, kids told to be quiet. You listen, then ask questions only what is important. I was thinking, "I going be the one to ask the kūpuna. If they no tell their stories, only going go with them to the graves." Plenty time I go ask, but they no like answer me. They only tell me, "Hoo, boy, you nīele, you nosey!"

I heard that around town, too. "Ho, that boy nīele." When I hear that, I go back to the kūpuna and I apologize, in Hawaiian, "Please excuse me. I not being nīele. I respect you. I just like know how you guys was feeling–from before." I gotta ask the question for get the knowledge.

I tell you one reason why I'm like that. Before me, my sister, Beatrice Kahilihiwa, came to Kalaupapa. She was sent from Kalihi Hospital in 1942. When I was in Honolulu, I only could see her in pictures. My parents would point to the picture and tell me, "That's your sister."

But I wanted to know more about my sister, you know. That's why when I wen' come Kalaupapa, I wen' ask. Although she had passed away I finally got to learn about her from the kūpuna like Tutu Louisa and Auntie Branco. The ones that wen' really open up to me was Aunty Helen Keao and Sara Meyer, because they was there same time as my sister. That was one important reason I wen' ask, and they wen' answer. Through them, I finally got my relationship with my sister that I wanted all my life. The spirit of my sister wen' live through the stories of the kūpuna.

If kūpuna and kids can make that kine relationship, can learn so much. ❖

Boogie Kahilihiwa was born in Kalapana on the Big Island. When he was nine years old, he was sent to Hale Mōhalu, the O'ahu Hansen's disease facility. In 1959, amid rumors that authorities might no longer place patients at Kalaupapa, Boogie knew he wanted to live there. That Christmas he got his wish and moved to Kalaupapa, where he kept busy working–joining the clean-up gang, painting and plumbing. Mainly, he loved to surf and dive in Kalaupapa's pristine waters. One of Boogie's fondest memories is of the time he got to surf Waikīkī with some of Hawaii's most famous beachboys.

Katherine Puahala
Kalaupapa Resident

"Something good can come out of nothing."

I was taken to Kalihi Hospital when I was only nine. When my father left me at the hospital, I just cried. I thought he didn't want me anymore. He didn't have a choice, of course. The doctors told him to take me to the hospital.

But I didn't understand this back then. I cry, cry, cry in bed by myself until, finally, a little girl came up to me and said, "You like play?" I looked at her and she look so kind, so I said, "Okay." The next thing I was playing with all these little kids. I don't know what would have happened to me if that little girl didn't come and take my hand that day.

Later, when my dad came back to visit, I remember thinking, "When you guys go leave?" I wanted to go back play with my friends. They were my new family–for the rest of my life. Later, after we were sent here to Kalaupapa, that little girl and I remain friends for the rest of our lives.

Slowly, me and my family not close like we should be. They come visit me, but they like strangers. The love is not genuine like it should be. We feel that way because we stayed apart for so long. Even they got scared of us. We was all brainwashed.

Of course, if they had the medicine back then this place wouldn't be here. Everybody would take the medicine and be well. It just came a little too late for some. It came a little too late for me. But I'm glad it came in the nick of time for the others and good luck for them that they got treated. That's life. You cannot hold grudge. Just be grateful for others getting ahead. And you just learn to live with it.

Life is not a bowl of cherries. There's a lot of sorrow. The main thing is you let the keikis know that they are loved, that this world is not all that bad. Look for the good parts. Something good can come out of anything. ❖

Katherine Puahala was nine years old when she was diagnosed with Hansen's disease and sent to Kalihi Hospital for confinement. She was sent to Kalaupapa in 1942 when she was 14. "When I came, we had 300 patients. But every day we had funeral. When you hear the church bell ring, somebody died. Sometimes two in one day, three one day. We were scared." Auntie Katherine and her husband, Jubilee, were married for nearly 50 years until his passing in 1997. "We had our ups and downs," she acknowledges, "but if you value your marriage, you keep working at it. Because who's perfect? Nobody's perfect."

Shannon Crivello
Kalaupapa's Chef

"That night I had a powerful nightmare that changed my life."

After I got out of high school, I got into drugs. It got so bad I eventually got fired from my job and kicked out of my apartment. One day, my brother Kawika came and confronted me. He told me I'd have to start my life all over again, but that only I could make that choice. It was hard, but I took it to heart–went to culinary arts school and turned my life around. I worked for some five-star hotels and even became head chef at one of them. But there's lots of cocaine and "ice" going around in some of those hotels, and I fell down again.

One day, at my mom's suggestion–she's like my guardian angel–I went to see a movie called "Once Were Warriors." That movie triggered memories I had chosen to block out for so many years–like a wall I built around me as a means of survival. The movie was about child abuse, alcohol, drugs, all the things that had happened in my childhood. I left feeling pretty restless, went home and finally fell asleep.

That night I had a powerful nightmare that changed my life. In my dream I'm sitting in the theater again, except I'm watching my own movie. I'm coming through my mom's womb, and I'm confronted by all the horrible things I had kept hidden for so long. In my dream I'm trying to escape, but I can't. Then I see a man with his back to me. As he turns around, I look into his eyes. It's my dad. He lunges at me as if to hit me, but he bites me in the stomach. That's when I woke up and I was holding my stomach, it was so sore. So I pulled up my shirt and there was a huge bite mark there! Then as I lifted my head, I saw a dark figure in the room. It drifted away.

I believe what happened that night was God's way of telling me, "Why are you running away? The hardships that happen to you, you create." I had to learn to accept my faults and not run from them. I believe God led me back here to Moloka'i–to find peace at Kalaupapa, so I could finally understand the beauty of things. ❖

Shannon Crivello was born and raised on Moloka'i. He boarded at Mid-Pacific Institute on O'ahu, where he played football for Pac Five. He also attended the University of Hawai'i-Hilo for two years, and later earned his degree in culinary arts. Shanon currently serves as Kalaupapa's chef. He also heads an organization for young leaders–Na Pua Nohi Na'auao (The Flowers of Enlightenment from Deep Within Ourselves)–dedicated to enhancing the spirit of the people of Moloka'i.

Index

Aloha has many meanings, many forms of expression. It is vital that we preserve it by passing it on to our children. *The Aloha Song* was written by my daughters, Erika-Rae, age 12, and Brooke Ligaya, age 9, with a little help from "Daddy" Noland.

The Aloha Song

I want to tell you how I am feeling
About this wonderful place
    we call Hawai'i
I want to tell you how I am feeling
About this magical place
It's for you and me

There are so many places I've been
But my favorite place is Hawai'i
Bright is the sky
    and the ocean so clear
This is the place that I love

I know sometimes that
    it's hard to live here
Everything is so expensive
But my daddy told me a long time ago
This is your place, it's your home

I know the people, often they wonder
How can we all live together
ALOHA is not
    just some words on a sign
It's something you feel from inside

So...I want to help you
    feel my Aloha
I know you can feel it like me
It's here in your heart

Words and music by Erika-Rae Conjugacion,
Brooke Ligaya Conjugacion and Brother Noland